Selected Poems of

John Oxenham

Selected Poems of John Oxenham

EDITED BY

CHARLES L. WALLIS

WITH A BIOGRAPHICAL SKETCH BY

ERICA OXENHAM

Biography Index Reprint Series

BOOKS FOR LIBRARIES PRESS
FREEPORT, NEW YORK

INTERNATIONAL STANDARD BOOK NUMBER:
0-8369-8103-0

LIBRARY OF CONGRESS CATALOG CARD NUMBER:
71-179735

PRINTED IN THE UNITED STATES OF AMERICA
BY
NEW WORLD BOOK MANUFACTURING CO., INC.
HALLANDALE, FLORIDA 33009

Acknowledgments

The editor wishes to express his appreciation to the following publishers for permission to reprint several of the poems appearing in this collection: American Tract Society, Doubleday & Company, Methuen & Co., Ltd., Methodist Book Concern, The Pilgrim Press; and to Messrs. Longmans Green & Co. for permission to use the material in the biographical sketch, from the book *J. O.*

Editor's Preface

Nearly one and a half million volumes of John Oxenham's verses have been published in England. Americans, for the most part, have known Mr. Oxenham by reputation alone. Although a number of his finest verses have been included in various anthologies of poetry, no copy of the poet's selected verses has hitherto been released in this country.

Friends of John Oxenham will find in this volume the familiar verses along with a wide selection of his most representative verses, arranged topically.

The interesting biographical sketch by Miss Erica Oxenham, the poet's daughter, is the fullest account of Mr. Oxenham's life printed in America. The editor is indebted to Miss Oxenham for making available all published verses and for the authority to include many heretofore unpublished manuscripts.

Contents

III. THE PILGRIM WAY

IV. BURDEN-BEARERS

V. WHEN HE TRIES THE HEARTS OF MEN

VI. THE CALL OF THE DEAD

VII. THE SACRAMENTS

VIII. SANCTUARY

"J. O."—A Biographical Sketch
by Erica Oxenham

My father's real name was William Arthur Dunkerley, and he did not adopt the nom de plume of John Oxenham until 1896. But I have referred to him throughout this sketch as J. O. to avoid confusion.

If anyone had told Mr. William Dunkerley, wholesale provision merchant of Manchester, that the son born to him on November 12, 1852, would become a writer whose books would be known in many parts of the world, he would have laughed. He himself read the Bible and the newspapers. His wife probably omitted the newspapers and substituted cookery books. How then did J. O. become a writer? He had no School of Journalism to help him, but he proved an apt and willing pupil in the harder but more effective School of Experience.

Though he did not realize it, the first step in J. O.'s training as a novelist began at school with his love of history, and it was continued when, after school and college, he went to France at the age of nineteen to take charge of the French branch of his father's business.

The French that he had learned at school seemed of little use to him, and it was essential that he should so master the language that he could conduct business in it. So the first few months were a time of hard and steady toil.

Once he had mastered French a full and very enjoyable life opened for him. With his headquarters at Rennes, he went up and down the country districts of Normandy and Brittany, interviewing farmers, buying their produce, and arranging for its shipment to England. "I am having rare times of it," he wrote home, "flying about the country like a whirlwind, sleeping at one town, breakfasting at a buffet on the line, dining at another town, sleeping at a third. It is fine and very jolly." Once he said that he thought he must have a well-developed *bump* of travel, "for I do delight in knocking about."

But his time in France did much more than give him an enjoyable life. It was the foundation of his career as a writer. To begin with, it gave him a thorough business training, and it was through the door of business that he later entered the literary world. But, more important still, it gave him the freedom of the Continent. Knowing French thoroughly, he had the passport into any country, for there were few places where either French or English would not take him. And, having to travel extensively in the youthful formative years, he learned the art of being at home in all surroundings. Then, too, his life at Rennes was somewhat lonely, with no companion of his own people at first; he had long winter evenings in which to read and study, and he soaked himself in the classics and in history. He had valuable opportunities of meeting and talking with men of various nationalities who stayed at his hotel, and so he absorbed other people's points of view. This gave him a wide understanding of their problems and resulted in a sympathy with no nationalistic bounds or limits. During those years there were few parts of the Continent he did not visit in the way of business, and he spent his holidays tramping in Switzerland and France and Italy with a knapsack.

Developments in his father's business, however, led to a complete change in his life, and, in 1877, he and his young wife set off for America. A branch of the business was opened in New York; the young couple settled down very happily in Orange, and joined Trinity Congregational Church in East

Orange. Everyone seems to have been very kind to them, and they made many friends. Indeed, there seemed every reason to expect that they were settled there for life, but business troubles hit the New York branch, and it had to be abandoned.

J. O. was loath to leave the New World and to return to the Old, so he looked around for other work. He decided to explore the possibilities of orange-growing and sheep-farming in Florida and Georgia. Although he knew nothing whatever about either of these, the prospect of a new and adventurous life attracted him so mightily that he set off full of hope and excitement.

Nothing came of the trip, however, except a number of amusing experiences. I think J. O. realized that the country was too rough and undeveloped for a young wife, and that it would not be fair to subject her to a lonely life there. So, reluctantly, he turned his face from the stimulating prospects of the New World, and I and the rest of the family just missed the opportunity of being born good Americans!

It was difficult to settle down into a humdrum groove in a provincial town. France, and then America, had wholly unfitted J. O. for it, and before long he was seeking new adventures. While in America he had read and enjoyed the *Detroit Free Press,* and he wrote to the editor suggesting the idea of an English edition. The editor replied that one of their staff, Robert Barr, had had the same idea, and was even then on his way to England to look into the possibilities. He cabled him to call on J. O., and out of that meeting came the English edition which ran merrily and profitably for about eight years. It was a great adventure, for neither Barr nor J. O. knew anything about publishing. But they learned by experience and made a success of it, Barr acting as editor, and J. O. as business manager.

One adventure led to another. An American watch company wanted its watch introduced into England, and sent a representative, armed with letters of introduction from the D. F. P. Headquarters, to discuss the matter with the London office. After much planning it was agreed to offer the watch, and a year's subscription to the paper, for 10/6d, and J. O. undertook some large-scale advertising. Many of his schemes were outstandingly spectacular, as for example when the company hired for the day of the Oxford and Cambridge Boat-race every steamboat on the Thames, and carried wearers of the watch to and from the course free of charge.

Fortunately developments in Fleet Street lured J. O. away from the fascinations of advertising. He and Barr started *The Idler,* a monthly magazine, and later J. O. and Jerome K. Jerome (author of *Three Men in a Boat*) produced a weekly paper, *To-Day.* In each case J. O. directed the business side, leaving the literary side to Barr and Jerome.

It was at this time that J. O. began to try his hand at writing. Reading one of the stories sent in to the magazines, he thought to himself, "I believe I could write as well as this myself!" And, when he began, he realized to his delight that he had a rich storehouse of memories waiting to be drawn upon. His adventures in France and Switzerland in the early days gave him unlimited material, and he was able to visualize places he had visited and people he had met in a way which made the descriptions of them a delight to his readers.

A new and fascinating hobby now opened for him. At first it *was* a hobby. He wrote short stories in the train on his way home from business, and found the doing of it a great refreshment to his mind. Still another asset of those early days, his love of history, now came into its own. Short stories, and then full-length novels, began to weave themselves around incidents of the Franco-Prussian War, of which he had heard at firsthand from the actual participants when he went to France in 1871. He relived their adventures with them, and, knowing intimately the places and the people, he pictured them so vividly that they came to life in his hands.

It was now that "John Oxenham" was born. J. O. was convinced that Fleet Street would not take him seriously as an author if he wrote under the name of W. A. Dunkerley, the well-known business manager, and he was determined to be taken seriously in what he now knew was his real vocation. So for a time the literary world knew both W. A. Dunkerley and John Oxenham, but the latter was never seen. Editors found that they could not interview him, and even correspondence with him was a lengthy business. It was understood that he lived in Scotland on the Clyde, and that he was frequently away on fishing expeditions. The real truth was that, to hide his identity, J. O. sent all his letters and messages from London to a sister-in-law in Greenock, and she repacked them and posted them to his agent in London. The agent replied to the Greenock address, and the letters were forwarded to J. O. in London.

The double identity led to many amusing experiences. Once an editor wrote that he was coming north to see the mysterious author, and J. O. received the letter just in time to wire asking him to postpone his visit. J. O. explained that he was three hundred miles from Greenock when the letter arrived, as indeed he was, for he was in London within a stone's throw of the editor's office!

There were some tantalizing incidents, too, as for example when J. O.'s own board of directors discussed the price to be paid to John Oxenham for a short story, and J. O., as a member of the board, had to agree, to his chagrin, to a sum lower than he had hoped to receive. The irony of the incident lay in the fact that, as managing director, J. O. was constantly urging economy on the board, and so he could hardly take the opposite line on that occasion.

Soon J. O. realized that he could not carry on the two

jobs satisfactorily, and that he must choose between them. John Oxenham was becoming well-known as a writer, and he needed more time to develop all the possibilities opening before him. So the business manager resigned, and W. A. Dunkerley disappeared from Fleet Street. But John Oxenham's name was seen in most of the monthly magazines, and on the covers of two novels a year for many years.

It was a wise choice. There was no doubt in his mind that writing was his chosen work, and he was entirely happy in it. He wrote, "I say deliberately that if I never sold a line the time I have spent in writing has been repaid many times over by the pleasure of it."

Although he found great happiness in the actual writing, these were anxious years. He wrote, "To become a successful writer a man needs not only to have the power to write, but much more the power to *wait*, and I am not sure that the latter is not the supreme test." There were tedious delays while editors and publishers made up their minds and a still longer delay while their accountants made up the books. J. O., with a young family of six, and with other responsibilities, could not afford to wait, and for many years he was haunted by the fear of financial failure. No wonder he wrote:

> I had done sums, and sums, and sums,
> Inside my aching head.
> I'd tried in vain to pierce the glooms
> That lay so thick ahead.
> But two and two will not make five,
> Nor will do when I'm dead.

But—and this is the important point—the title of that poem which begins, "I faced a future all unknown," is "God Is Good."

That was his sheet-anchor all through life. Without that strong and firm faith he never could have fought his way through the difficulties of those early years. But his faith, his belief in himself, and the unswerving confidence of his wife, carried him on, and in time John Oxenham had an established place in the literary world.

The life of a novelist, too, had many compensations which business life—even with a comfortable and regular salary—had denied him. "You can carry your work under your own hat, and be responsible to nobody," he wrote. That was one great asset. He was free and his own master.

Another asset which he valued greatly was the ability to travel, and travel was always to him an essential part of the novelist's equipment. Though his early experiences had provided the foundations of his literary career, he could not live entirely on the past. He must refresh his mind and his memory by revisiting the places about which he was writing, and by exploring new ones. So he went for long holidays to the Continent and to the Channel Islands, living cheaply and working hard at a manuscript. He returned reinvigorated to the concentrated effort which all his books received before they went to the publishers. He made his books as flawless as possible, going over them eight or ten times before they went to the typist, and then again, and still again, when they appeared in proof.

J. O. was at his best on holiday. Two of his chief characteristics were his interest in people and his zest for life. Both had full play on holiday. It was the simple people in whom he was interested, and, in the little French village where he and I went each summer for many years, he was a welcome guest in many tiny cottage homes. Speaking French naturally and easily, he was able to share in the people's interests, their work, their hopes and ambitions for their children, their worries and anxieties. And it was no perfunctory interest; one had the feeling that he was absorbed in their problems and that they were as vital to him as to them.

And his zest for life! J. O. would never miss any excitement that was on foot, Bastille Day, the Fêtes, firework displays, village sports. When we were children, he took us to every circus and fair that came to the neighborhood.

So, in a patchwork of light and shade, great happiness, and a background of anxiety, J. O. spent the next phase of his literary life.

John Oxenham the novelist was now successfully launched on his career, but all the time still another identity was quietly building itself up in the background. This was John Oxenham the poet, or, as he put it, John Oxenham the writer of verses. He was modest about his verses, and always affirmed that he was not "aspiring to the laurels of a poet."

From time to time, for many years, verses had formed themselves in his brain, and had buzzed there like bees until he wrote them down. It was a collection of these verses which appeared in 1913 in a little book called *Bees in Amber*. His publishers were horrified that a well-known novelist should suddenly turn to the writing of poetry, and refused the book. Whereupon J. O. undertook the printing and production of it himself, and they reluctantly agreed to publish it. To their great surprise it was warmly welcomed, and, with the outbreak of the first World War in the following year, the book soon became an outstanding success. It appealed both to the men at the front and to their friends left lonely at home, with the result that, during the war years, 228,000 copies were sold. A much larger circulation was enjoyed by the volumes of verses which followed.

J. O.'s success as a writer of verses came, I believe, because he spoke as an ordinary everyday man, and so all men listened to him. He spoke from the heart, and his verses are himself—simple, unpretentious, deeply rooted in the things of the spirit. The verses are the "essence" of J. O.

J. O. emphasized the idea that there must be the urge to write, whether novels or verses, or the work would not be worth the doing. He encouraged aspiring authors who had that urge, and was dissuasive toward dilettante ones. I found the following among his papers:

> Write if you must,
> But—think on this—
> Christ wrote but once
> And then in dust.

After the first World War J. O.'s career took a new turn. Just as the businessman was superseded by the novelist, and the novelist by the poet, so now the poet gave place to the writer of religious books. J. O. embarked on the most important phase of his literary work.

All his life he had wished to write a life of Jesus. There are many beginnings among his papers, but until this time only one had reached any considerable length, and it was unfinished.

An American friend turned J. O.'s thoughts once again in that direction. A short story of J. O.'s had been published as a small book entitled *The Cedar Box*. It described an imaginary incident in Christ's boyhood, and the American friend wrote enthusiastically about it. The man who could write that, he said, could write about the early days of Christ's life in a way that would live.

It was the spur J. O. needed. He started again with zest, and this time the story "just flowed out." "The story wrote itself," he said. "I simply acted as scribe putting it down on paper as it came."

It was published in 1925 under the title of *The Hidden Years*, and it is still selling and still bringing appreciative letters from all parts of the world. The New York *Sun* in a review said, "There are consummate works of art that appear just to have happened. This is one of them."

The Hidden Years was followed by other books dealing

xxiii

with the life of Christ and with the work of the apostles after Pentecost. They found an appreciative and grateful public.

Just as the verses appealed to the ordinary man and woman because they were not "highbrow," so the religious books appealed to them because were not theological. They told a clear and simple story, and through it they carried a direct message to the hearts of their readers.

J. O. had received many warm and grateful letters from the readers of his verses to whom he had brought comfort and hope in the darkest days of their lives. Now he received many more from those whose faith he had relit, and, as he always replied, many of his readers thought of him as a personal friend. They wrote to him about their difficulties and their anxieties, sure that he would understand and sympathize. And J. O. always did understand and sympathize in a remarkable way. "You are one of those most Blessed Ones," wrote one, "who see and bring out all that is best in your fellow-beings." And another, "They haven't invented the kind of doctorate worthy to bestow upon you yet, but I suggest that you should be called 'Doctor of Humanity.' "

His interest in people was so real and so individual that it evoked a warm affection in return. One evidence of this was the wide use of his nickname of "J. O." and people adopted it almost unconsciously, as though they found "Mr. Oxenham" much too formal. Others called him "Father John." One woman wrote, "I don't know how to tell you what the richness of your friendship has done for me. I call you Father John because, through you, that great word has been filled with new content. I now call God Father, but I could not do that till I knew you. The word held fear. Now I begin to know the Fatherhood of God."

These friendships meant much to J. O. and, as the years drew on, he dwelt increasingly in the lives of his friends, sharing with them the active adventures which were drawing to a close for him. It seemed as though his friends were in his mind all the time. He was constantly thinking of them. An article in the paper, a picture, a poem, would be marked for this one and that. These were little things in themselves, but in the sum of them they spoke of a mind and a heart big enough to have many compartments for his friends, each one individual and clear. To J. O. each of these personal threads was unique, a link between their two selves, distinct and personal.

One would have expected that, after a busy, energetic life, the advancing years would have irked him, and that he would have found life dull and tedious. But he did not. He had the capacity to adapt himself readily to new places and new conditions, and, in 1938, when a severe attack of bronchitis warned him that his traveling days were over, he settled down with great happiness in a small bungalow on the South Downs overlooking the sea. There he was content to sit back and rest, knowing that he had done his best, both for us and for the world. He had a full and busy life. He had published forty-four novels, ten books of verse, and a number of books on religious themes. Now he appreciated the fact that the bustle and battle of life were over for him. He wrote:

> By God's good Grace
> My race I ran,
> And now lie here
> A Grateful Man.

Gratitude was a virtue J. O. had always possessed; it was abundantly in evidence in these later years. He was appreciative of the smallest service in a way which made one want to earn the thanks he so gratefully expressed.

Those last years were not idle. Two books appeared in 1940, and on another he was busy until three days before he passed on in 1941. That was how he had always hoped it would be; he had always dreaded the thought of being past work.

> Lord, when Thou seest that my work is done,
> Let me not linger on,
> With failing powers,
> Adown the weary hours,—
> A workless worker in a world of work.
> But, with a word,
> Just bid me home,
> And I will come
> Right gladly,—
> Yea, right gladly
> Will I come.

Among the many jottings I found when he had passed on was this, "Thanks be to God for a life full packed, with things that matter crying to be done—a life, thank God, of never-ending strife against odds . . . Just time enough to do one's best, and then to pass on, leaving the rest to Him . . ."

I

God's Friendly Hand

God's Friendly Hand

One way there is—one only way—
Which makes you strong to overcome
Life's evils and the blows of fate,
And, in the end, to bring you home.

God's friendly hand is seeking yours,
Grip hold of it and clasp it tight!
His love all ills and bruises cures
His strength will help you win your fight.

God's Handwriting

He writes in characters too grand
For our short sight to understand;
We catch but broken strokes, and try
To fathom all the mystery
Of withered hopes, of death, of life,
The endless war, the useless strife,—
But there, with larger, clearer sight,
We shall see this—His way was right.

Giant Circumstance

Though every nerve be strained
To fine accomplishment,
Full oft the life falls spent
Before the prize is gained.
And, in our discontent
At waste so evident,
In doubt and vast discouragement
We wonder what is meant.
But, tracing back, we find
A Power that held the ways—
A Mighty Hand, a Master Mind,
That all the troubled course defined,
And overruled the days.
Some call it Fate; some—Chance;
Some—Giant Circumstance;
And some, upreaching to the sense
Of God within the circumstance,
Do call it—Providence!

In Silence and in Quietness

In silence and in quietness
God's mighty works are wrought,
Unheard, unseen, His workmanship
Is to perfection brought.

Deep in the earth, and high above,
His unknown powers display

Their multiform activities,
And all creation sway.

Ever at work, unheard, unseen,
He is, in everything,
Cause and effect at once in all
That is or e'er has been.

Help us, O Lord, in quietness
To do our work, like Thee,
And our souls brace with Thy sweet grace
Of high tranquillity!

from In All Thy Hidden Workings

The Pruner

God is a zealous pruner,
For He knows—
Who, falsely tender, spares the knife
But spoils the rose.

In the Wilderness

In sore distress,
I stumbled in the wilderness;
No help was nigh,
No answer to my cry.
Great was my bitterness,—

I was alone,
My strength all gone;
And I was sore afraid
And wished me dead,
So heavy on me lay the rod.
Then, in my fear,
I raised my head,
And there—
Found God.

Flighting Wings

The mother eagle wrecks the nest
To make her fledglings fly,
But watches each, with wings outstretched,
And fierce maternal eye;
And swoops if any fail to soar,
And lands them on the crag once more.

So God at times breaks up our nest,
Lest, sunk in slothful ease,
Our souls' wings moult and lose the zest
For battle with the breeze;
But ever waits, with arms of love,
To bear our souls all ills above.

On Eagles' Wings
(A Verse for a Pilot)

Supremely in His Hand are you,
To whom the mighty joy is given
On eagles' wings to climb the blue,
And, on the pinions of the winds,
To sweep the boundless plains of heaven.
So—to your minds
Be present this,
For cheer in your necessities,—

Who swings the countless spheres in space,
Yet to their even courses holds;
Who set the firmament in place
And its infinitudes unfolds,—
Come what come may of hap or chance,
He is your sure deliverance.

If but as Pilot by your side
He sits, upon Whose breath you ride,
He shall preserve you from alarms,
Spread wide His everlasting arms,
And bear you safely up on high
In His most noble company.

No sparrow falls but it is known
Of Him who sits on Heaven's high throne;
And you, in your supremest hour,
Shall feel the uplift of His power,
And know you're not alone.

Quoted in part

Props

Earthly props are useless,
 On Thy grace I fall;
Earthly strength is weakness,
 Father, on Thee I call,—
 For comfort, strength, and guidance,
 O, give me all!

Bed-Rock

I have been tried,
Tried in the fire,
And I say this,
As the result of dire distress,
And tribulation sore—
That a man's happiness doth not consist
Of that he hath, but of the faith
And trust in God's great love
These bring him to.
Nought else is worth consideration
For the peace a man may find
In perfect trust in God
Outweighs all else, and is
The only possible foundation
For true happiness.

God Is Good

I faced a future all unknown,
No opening could I see,
I heard without the night wind moan,
The ways were dark to me,—
"I cannot face it all alone
O be Thou near to me!"

I had done sums, and sums, and sums,
Inside my aching head.
I'd tried in vain to pierce the glooms
That lay so thick ahead.
But two and two will not make five,
Nor will do when I'm dead.

And then I thought of Him who fed
Five thousand hungry men,
With five small casual loaves of bread,—
Would he were here again!—
Dear God! hast Thou still miracles
For the troubled sons of men?

He has, He will, He worketh still,
In ways most wonderful.
He drew me from the miry clay,
He filled my cup quite full.
And while my heart can speak I'll tell
His love unspeakable.

"Rest in the Lord!"—I saw it there,
On the tablets of the night.
And, comforted, I dropped my care

Where burdens have no weight.
Then, trustfully, I turned and slept,
And woke, and it was light.

God works to-day as He did of old
For the lightening of men's woes.
His wonders never can be told,
His goodness no man knows,—
His Love, His Power, His Tenderness,—
Nor shall do till life's close.

His kindness is so very great,
His greatness is so good.
He looks upon my low estate,
He gives me daily food.
And nothing is too small for Him,—
Yes, truly! God is good.

All's Well!

Is the pathway dark and dreary?
    God's in His heaven!
Are you broken, heart-sick, weary?
    God's in His heaven!
Dreariest roads shall have an ending,
Broken hearts are for God's mending.
        All's well! All's well!
        All's . . . . well!

Is the burden past your bearing?
    God's in His heaven!

10

Hopeless?—Friendless?—No one caring?
  God's in His heaven!
Burdens shared are light to carry,
Love shall come though long he tarry.
    All's well! All's well!
    All's . . . . well!

Is the light for ever failing?
  God's in His heaven!
Is the faint heart ever quailing?
  God's in His heaven!
God's strong arms are all around you,
In the dark He sought and found you.
    All's well! All's well!
    All's . . . . well!

Is the future black with sorrow?
  God's in His heaven!
Do you dread each dark to-morrow?
  God's in His heaven!
Nought can come without His knowing,
Come what may 'tis His bestowing.
    All's well! All's well!
    All's . . . . well!

           Quoted in part

His Mercy Endureth Forever

Our feet have wandered, wandered far and wide,—
His mercy endureth for ever!
From that strait path in which the Master died,—
His mercy endureth for ever!
Low have we fallen from our high estate,
Long have we lingered, lingered long and late;
But the tenderness of God
Is from age to age the same,
And His Mercy endureth for ever!

There is no sin His Love can not forgive;—
His mercy endureth for ever!
No soul so stained His Love will not receive;
His mercy endureth for ever!
No load of sorrow but His touch can move,
No hedge of thorns that can withstand His Love;
For the tenderness of God
Is from age to age the same,
And His Mercy endureth for ever!

So we will sing, whatever may betide;—
His mercy endureth for ever!
Nought but ourselves can keep us from His side;—
His mercy endureth for ever!
What though no place we win in life's rough race,
Our loss may prove the measure of His grace.
For the tenderness of God
Is from age to age the same,
And His Mercy endureth for ever!

The Spread Table

Where'er I be, Lord, spread for me
Thy table with its holy fare,
Then, though my lot be slenderness,
And my tent but the wilderness,
Full amply plenished I shall be,
                    Since Thou art there.

And wilt Thou break the bread for me?
For me pour out the sacred wine?
And as we eat and drink wilt Thou
Renew in me the holy vow,
And fill me with new love for Thee,
                    Since I am Thine?

Not the spread table, nor the wine,
Nor the sweet breaking of the bread,
That makes the feast,—but that we meet
Together here in commune sweet
With Thee, and by Thy Grace Divine,
                    We all are fed.

And when we leave Thy table, Lord,
And go into the world again,
Help us to carry with us there
The savour of that holy fare,
And prove the virtue of The Word
                    To other men.

The City of God

Where shall the City of God be found?
  —In some vague place beyond the sky,
  Enshrined in mystic mystery?
  —In some far, dim futurity?
  Embalmed in hopes of prophecy?

Not there shall the City of God be found,
But—
        In every land where Peace doth reign,
        And Faith and Hope full growth attain,
        And Love turns Life to noblest gain,—
                There the City of God is.

        In every home where God abides,
        And over all its life presides,
        And its fair doings rules and guides,—
                There the City of God is.

        In every heart where holy fires,
        Fanned by the love which never tires,
        Kindle sweet thoughts to high desires,—
                There the City of God is.

        Wherever man doth heavenward turn,
        And in all life doth Thee discern,
        And feels Thy Love within him burn,—
                There the City of God is.

        Not alone in the heavens above,
        But everywhere in the heart of Love,—
                There the City of God is.

The Word of God

Thy Word is Light—Thy Saving Grace
Upon a troubled world outpoured;
For its fair guidance in our night,
With grateful hearts, we thank Thee, Lord.

Thy Word is Truth—the Truth that burns,
And breaks, and binds, and sets men free.
Now let Thy Truth sweep through the world
And bring its wayward heart to Thee.

Thy Word is Life—abounding Life,
That quickens body, mind, and soul,
And gives new meaning to our lives,
And sets Thy seal upon the whole.

Thy word is Promise of the Dawn
That shall bring in Thy Glorious Day,
When all creation shall rejoice
To do Thy Will and own Thy sway.

Thy Word is Love—the Love that was,
And is, and evermore shall be;
Love, the Beginning; Love, the End;
Love, timeless as eternity.

For that great Love, unbounded, free,
That binds us with a golden cord
To one another and to Thee,
We thank Thee, thank Thee, thank Thee, Lord!

Thank God for Opened Eyes

Thank God for opened eyes,
And hearts not too o'erwhelmed
With worldly snares and earthly cares
For His immanencies!

To find Him everywhere,
In every smallest thing,
Is His good gift man's soul to lift
Above its earthly fare.

To trace His delicate
Fine craftsmanship in all,
Gives sense of new-born reverence
For all things small and great.

In all things Him we find,
If we but bring to all,
With conscious will and loving zeal,
An open heart and mind.

from In Nature's Wonders

Shut Windows
(For the Braille Magazine)

When the outer eye grows dim,
Turns the inner eye to Him,
  Who makes darkness light.
Fairer visions you may see,

Live in nobler company,
And in larger liberty,
    Than the men of sight.

He sometimes shuts the windows but to open
    hidden doors,
Where all who will may wander bold and free,
For His house has many mansions, and the
    mansions many floors,
And every room is free to you and me.

As Christ Was Then

As Christ was then, so God is now,
Tender, loving, true.
Friend of friends to the men of old,
So will He be to you.

I

Let All Men Everywhere Praise God

Let all men everywhere praise God
For His most fair creation;
And praise still more the Open Door
That offers man salvation!

Let all men everywhere praise God
For His Son's sacrificing!

17

That through His Own He hath made known
His mercy all sufficing.

Praise God all creatures everywhere
For mercies so unbounded!—
No thing there is but ever is
By His great love surrounded.

from In Times and Seasons

II

Let All Men Everywhere Praise God

Let all men everywhere praise God
For all that He hath done,
But most of all for Love's High Call
Through Jesus Christ, His Son!
To Him all praise and glory be
While Time its course doth run!
To Him the Kingdom and the Power,
When Time and Everness once more
For evermore are one!

Some—and Some

Some have much, and some have more,
Some are rich, and some are poor,
Some have little, some have less,
Some have not a cent to bless
Their empty pockets, yet possess
True riches in true happiness.

To some—unclouded skies and sunny days,
To some—gray weather and laborious ways,
To all—Thy grace,
To those who fall—Thy tenderness!

II

The Eternal Christ

The Eternal Christ

Our God is an eternal Christ,
Unchangeable, unchanged.
His Love is still as warm and true
As when life's common ways He ranged
Beneath the Syrian blue.

Our God is an eternal Christ,
And Christ is Very Love,—
The Love that, ere the world was made,
He with His justice interwove,
As He the way surveyed.

Our God is an eternal Christ,
All tender, wise, and true,
As once He was to those of old,
So is He now to me and you,
Till all the tale is told.

As Christ was then, so God is now,
A wise and loving friend.
No feeblest cry will He deny,
But of His best will surely send,
And that right instantly.

The Christ

The good intent of God became the Christ.
And lived on earth—the Living Love of God,
That men might draw to closer touch with
  heaven,
Since Christ in all the ways of man hath trod.

The High Things

The Greatest Day that ever dawned,—
It was a Winter's Morn.

The Finest Temple ever built
Was a Shed where a Babe was born.

The Sweetest Robes by woman wrought
Were the Swaths by the Baby worn.

And the Fairest Hair the world has seen,
—Those Locks that were never shorn.

The Noblest Crown man ever wore,—
It was the Plaited Thorn.

The Grandest Death man ever died,—
It was the Death of Scorn.

The Sorest Grief by woman known
Was the Mother-Maid's forlorn.

The Deepest Sorrows e'er endured
Were by The Outcast borne.

The Truest Heart the world e'er broke
Was the Heart by man's sins torn.

Where Christ Is Born Again

Wherever one repenting soul
Prays, in its agonies of pain,
By God's sweet grace to be made whole,—
  There, Christ is born again.

Wherever—bond of ancient thrall—
A strong soul bursts its shackling chain,
And upward strains to meet the call,—
  There, Christ is born again.

Wherever vision of the Light
Disturbs the sleeping souls of men,
Night trails away its shadowy flight,—
  And Christ is born again.

Wherever soul in travail turns,
And climbs the barriers that constrain,
With steady cheer Hope's sweet lamp burns,—
  And Christ is born again.

Where one foul thing is purged away,
And Life delivered of one stain,
Love rims with gold the coming day,—
  And Christ is born again.

The Inn of Life

As it was in the Beginning,—
Is Now,—
And . . . . ?

Anno Domini I

"No room!
No room!
The Inn is full,
Yea—overfull.
No room have we
For such as ye—
Poor folk of Galilee,
Pass on! Pass on!"

"Nay then!—
Your charity
Will ne'er deny
Some corner mean,
Where she may lie unseen.
For see!—
Her time is nigh."

"Alack! And she
So young and fair!
Place have we none;
And yet—how bid ye gone?
Stay then—out there
Among the beasts
Ye may find room,
And eke a truss
To lie upon."

Anno Domini 1913, etc., etc.
                  "No   room!
                   No room!
No room for Thee,
Thou Man of Galilee!
The house is full,
Yea, overfull.
There is no room for Thee,—
                  Pass on! Pass on!

Nay—see!
The place is packed.
We scarce have room
For our own selves,
So how shall we
Find room for Thee,
Thou Man of Galilee,—
                  Pass on! Pass on!

But—if Thou shouldst
This way again,
And we can find
So much as one small corner
Free from guest,
Not then in vain
Thy quest.
But now—
The house is full.
                  Pass on!"

Christ passes
On His ceaseless quest,
Nor will He rest
With any,
Save as Chiefest Guest.

My Guest

Within my holy place
My Chiefest One is dwelling,
Not as a passing guest
But of His own houseling.
O, miracle of grace,
My whole heart's love compelling—
Within this tiny space
The Lord of all Good Life,
The Very Light of Life and Love
Is dwelling!
And now my happy tears
Have washed away my fears,
And, past all mortal telling,
Within my heart the tide of Love
To fullest flood is welling.

Praise be to Thee!
To Thee unending praise,
For all the glowing depth and height
Of these God-given days!
For Thy sweet grace
Which in this place
Doth time and space alike efface,
And, merging faith in heavenly sight,
Dares, with its inner mystic light,
To look upon Thy face.

The Prince of Life

O, Prince of Life, Thy Life hath tuned
All life to sweeter, loftier grace!
Life's common rounds have wider bounds,
Since Thou hast trod life's common ways.

O, Heart of Love! Thy Tenderness
Still runs through life's remotest vein;
And lust and greed and soulless creed
Shall never rule the world again.

O Life of Love!—The Good Intent
Of God to man made evident,—
All down the years, despite men's fears,
Thy Power is still omnipotent.

O Life! O Love! O Living Word!—
Rent Veil, revealing God to man,—
Help, Lord! Lest I should crucify,
By thought or deed, Thy Love again.

Come Unto Me

Come unto Me, all you heavily burdened ones!
Come unto Me, all you weary ones, come!
The home is all waiting that I have prepared for you,
All through the years while I waited and cared for you,
And now I am waiting to welcome you home.
Come to Me! Come to Me! Come to Me! Come!
And you shall find rest for your souls!

Have I not borne greater burdens of sorrow?
Have I not known what it was to be lonely?
Lean on me now for to-day and to-morrow,
Trust in Me wholly, and trust in Me only!—
And you shall find rest for your souls!

Here for your sorrow is healing and gladness,
Give Me your burden, and take you another's,
So shall you rid you of all your own sadness,
Healing your own wound by healing your brother's,
And you shall find rest for your souls!

from Chaos and the Way Out

Road-Mates

From deepest depth, O Lord, I cry to Thee.
  "My Love runs quick to your necessity."

I am bereft; my soul is sick with loss.
  "Dear one, I know. My heart broke on the Cross."

What most I loved is gone. I walk alone.
  "My Love shall more than fill his place, my own."

The burden is too great for me to bear.
  "Not when I'm here to take an equal share."

The road is long, and very wearisome.
  "Just on in front I see the light of home."

The night is black; I fear to go astray.
  "Hold my hand fast. I'll lead you all the way."

My eyes are dim, with weeping all the night.
"With one soft kiss I will restore your sight."

And Thou wilt do all this for me?—*for me?*
"For this I came—to bear you company."

Quo Vadis?

Peter, outworn,
And menaced by the sword,
Shook off the dust of Rome;
And, as he fled,
Met one, with eager face,
Hastening cityward.
And, to his vast amaze,
It was the Lord.

    "Lord, whither goest Thou?"
He cried, importunate;
And Christ replied,—
    "Peter, I suffer loss.
    I go to take thy place,
    To bear thy cross."

Then Peter bowed his head,
Discomforted;
There at the Master's feet,
Found grace complete,
And courage, and new faith,
And turned—with Him,
To Death.

So we,—
Whene'er we fail
Of our full duty,
Cast on Him our load,—
On Him who suffered sore for us,
On Him who frail flesh wore for us,
On Him who all things bore for us,—
On Christ, the Lord.

Paul

Bond-slave to Christ, and in my bonds rejoicing,
　Earmarked to Him I counted less than nought;
His man henceforward, eager to be voicing
　That wondrous Love which Saul the Roman sought.

Sought him and found him, working bitter sorrow;
　Found him and claimed him, chose him for his own;
Bound him in darkness, till the glorious morrow
　Unsealed his eyes to that he had not known.

Gadara, A.D. 31

Rabbi, begone! Thy powers
Bring loss to us and ours.
Our ways are not as Thine.
Thou lovest men, we—swine.
Oh, get you hence, Omnipotence,
And take this fool of Thine!
His soul? What care we for his soul?
What good to us that Thou hast made him whole,
Since we have lost our swine?

And Christ went sadly.
He had wrought for them a sign
Of Love, and Hope, and Tenderness divine;
They wanted—swine.
Christ stands without *your* door and gently knocks;
But if your gold, or swine, the entrance blocks,
He forces no man's hold—he will depart,
And leave you to the treasures of your heart.

No cumbered chamber will the Master share,
But one swept bare
By cleansing fires, then plenished fresh and fair
With meekness, and humility, and prayer.
There will He come, yet, coming, even there
He stands and waits, and will no entrance win
Until the latch be lifted from within.

His Simple Creed

He taught them his new simple law
Of Right 'twixt God and man,
And showed them how from that would grow
Right too 'twixt man and man.

—That every man should strive his best
To serve his neighbour's need;—
"God first, then man—serve all you can!"
That was his simple creed.

—That none should ever have to ask
His neighbour's aid in vain,
But that his need itself should plead
And instant help obtain.

He taught that every man should do
As he would be done by,
For as man gives so he receives,
With utmost equity.

Give love and love will fill your life;
Give hate and hate is yours;
For as you give, so you receive,
And shall while life endures.

from His Way

He—They—We

They hailed Him King as He passed by,
They strewed their garments in the road,
But they were set on earthly things,
And He on God.

They sang His praise for that He did,
But gave His message little thought;
They could not see that their souls' good
Was all He sought.

They could not understand why He,
With powers so vast at His command,
Should hesitate to claim their rights
And free the land.

Their own concerns and this world's hopes
Shut out the wonder of His news;
And we, with larger knowledge, still
His Way refuse.

He walks among us still, unseen,
And still points out the only way,
But we still follow other gods
And Him betray.

The Wandering Jew

"Go quicker, Jesus!"
Kartaphilos said,
And smote The Prisoner on the head,
As He left the Judgment Hall.

"I go!" The Christ replied,
"But thou . . . for that foul blow,—
Linger thou here upon this side,
Until I bid thee go!"

And so,—through all centuries since then,
Undying, Kartaphilos drags his chain
Of lengthening years the wide world over,
Weary and fain;
Soul-shrunken, life's lamp dim,
He craves sweet Death, but all in vain;
Death passes by with cold disdain,
And will have none of him.

Hungering for that which most men dread,
He dies not, nor can die,
Until the Lord Christ come again
To loose his misery.

Nought dies—thought, word, or deed, once given,
Lives on and on and makes for hell or heaven.

"Lord, Is It I?"

One in the darkness wanders wide
The dim lands where the shadows hide,
Follows false fires, and far from home,
Dwells with the things that creep and roam;
And though Love calls makes no reply.—
      "Lord, is it I?"

And one in Primrose Paths doth stray,
Content with pleasures of the day,
Culls the fair flowers that fade and die,
And, heeding not that night is nigh,
Seeks but his sense to satisfy,—
      "Lord, is it I?"

And one did set to climb the hill,
But wearied of his better will,
And ere half-way he laid him down,—
So sore the cross, so far the crown,
While on himself he did rely.—
      "Lord, is it I?"

And one doth bravely breast the height
Where Faith and Hope are blessed with Sight,
And, casting all his burden on
The steps that lead up to the throne,
He to his Father draweth nigh.—
      "Lord, is it I?"

     The Master bowed
     His thorn-crowned head
     And said no word.
     But each one heard
     The Voice within him,—
      "Thou hast said!"

The Cross of Calvary

The Cross of Calvary
Was verily The Key
By which our Brother Christ
Unlocked The Door
Of Immortality
To you and me;
And, passing through Himself before,
He set it wide
For evermore,
That we, by His grace justified,
And by His great love fortified,
Might enter in all fearlessly,
And dwell for ever by His side.

from The Key

The Two Views

To man, it seemed that Evil had prevailed,
That His fair life had altogether failed,
And nought was left but what the Cross impaled;—
　　　　　　　But God saw otherwise!

They would have hailed Him King, and with acclaim,
Upon the wings of His far-reaching fame,
Have swept the land like a devouring flame;
　　　　　　　But God saw otherwise!

38

It seemed as though His life had gone for nought,—
Nothing to show for that long battle fought,
But a pale prisoner to the gibbet brought;—
                    But God saw otherwise!

We too, at times, come nigh to lose our hope,
When with life's evils we no more can cope,
And in the dark with heavy hearts we grope;
                    But God sees otherwise!

                              Quoted in part

Kinsman!—Canst Thou Forget?

I love to think upon Thy human need,
Thy baby fingers groping for the breast,
Thy white limbs on Thy mother's knee astrid,
Thy soft head croodling down into its nest.

I love to think upon those hidden years,
When just a boy Thou wast, with other boys,—
Sharing their hopes, their ventures, and their fears,
And jubilant with them in all their joys.

I love to think on Thy humanity,
Seeking God's Way, with ever-opening eyes,
Through the thronged courts of earthly vanity,
To that last crowning grace of sacrifice.

I love to think upon Thy dust-stained feet,
That ached and hardened with the stony road,
And craved relief from parch of noonday heat
In each cool stream that by the wayside flowed.

39

I love to think upon Thy needfulness,
That made the sinner's kiss upon Thy feet
Balm for old Simon's lack of heedfulness,
And to Thy want a joy most exquisite.

I love to think upon Thy human-ness
That welcomed sundown and the close of day,
Which left Thee free, for just a little space,
To climb the hill, and sit, and think, and pray.

I love Thy craving for sweet loneliness,
When the strain grew past human strength to bear,
I love Thy gracious calm amid the stress,
Yea—and the anguish of Thy last despair.

Though Thou was God, yet truly wast Thou man,—
Man like myself, since Thou life's round hast trod;
So, by Thy human sufferings, I can
Claim Thee as Brother yet acclaim Thee God.

Forget, Thou canst not.—God Thou art and man.
Thou too hast borne the yoke and kissed the rod.
By that, O Kinsman, to the full I can
Feel Thee my Brother, Father, Mother,—God.

Must Christ Still Wander

Must Christ still wander on unknown
As in the past?
Or—recognised—still left alone,
Despised—outcast?

Return!

We pray—
*"Lord Christ, come down again,
And dwell with us, the sons of men!"*

Yet why?
Not for His coming need we pray,
Since He is with us, night and day;
Closer than breath, than life, than death,
Our Lord is here,—
Is waiting, waiting, sad and lonely,
Waiting ever, waiting only
Till, with vision clear,
We shall forsake our devious ways,
And come in from the wilderness
To claim His proffered grace.

See Him—sad and lonely, waiting—
For our coming only waiting—
While, with wilful heart, we still
Go wandering down the flowery ways,
And seek our good in every place
Save where is righteousness;
And still elect the lower part,
Lest our own lower selves we thwart
And make our pleasures less.

Yes, surely Christ is with us now
As truly as when, long ago,
He put aside His high estate,
And lived man's life below,
And, dying, left His proxy meet,—
His fuller Self, His Comfort Sweet,—

His Advocate, the Paraclete,
To make His Love complete.

Not—"*God to men*
     Return!"
But—"*Man to God*
     Return!"—
Is man's one need to-day.
O, sons of men, and sons of God,
The Son of Man, the Son of God
Stands waiting for you in the Way;—
Heart, life, and soul,
He claims you whole,—
To-Day,—To-Day,—To-Day!

> *Return! Return!*
> *To Him again,*
> *Ye sons of men,*
>   *Return!*
> *To Him Who grace alone can give,—*
> *To Him through Whom alone we live,—*
>   *Return! Return!*

Our Only Hope

And will Thy feet once more be set
As once before—on Olivet?
And shall we recognise Thee then
Or blindly crucify again
          Our Only Hope?

O Come!—in whatsoever guise
And stand before our opened eyes,
Our Saviour Lord, our Christ, our King,
And to our desolation bring
                    Our Only Hope.

Live Christ

Live Christ!—and though thy way may be
In this world's sight adversity,
He who doth heed thy every need
Shall give thy soul prosperity.

Live Christ!—and though thy path may be
The narrow street of poverty,
He had not where to lay His Head
Yet lived in largest liberty.

Live Christ!—and though thy road may be
The strait way of humility,
He who first trod that way of God
Will clothe thee with His dignity.

Live Christ!—and though thy life may be
In much a valedictory,
The heavy cross brings seeming loss
But wins the crown of victory.

Live Christ!—and all thy life shall be
A High Way of Delivery,—
A Royal Road of goodly deeds,
Gold-paved with sweetest charity.

Live Christ!—and all thy life shall be
A sweet uplifting ministry,
A sowing of the fair white seeds
That fruit through all eternity.

Credo

Not what, but *Whom*, I do believe,
  That, in my darkest hour of need,
  Hath comfort that no mortal creed
  To mortal man may give;—
Not what, but *Whom!*
  For Christ is more than all the creeds,
  And His full life of gentle deeds
  Shall all the creeds outlive.
Not what I do believe, but *Whom!*
  Who walks beside me in the gloom?
  Who shares the burden wearisome?
  Who all the dim way doth illume,
  And bids me look beyond the tomb
  The larger life to live?—
Not what I do believe,
But *Whom!*
Not what,
But *Whom!*

III

The Pilgrim Way

The Pilgrim Way

But once I pass this way,
And then—no more.
But once—and then, the Silent Door
Swings on its hinges,—
Opens . . . . closes,—
And no more
I pass this way.
So while I may,
With all my might,
I will essay
Sweet comfort and delight,
To all I meet upon the Pilgrim Way.
For no man travels twice
The Great Highway,
That climbs through Darkness up to Light,—
Through Night
To Day.

The Ways

To every man there openeth
A Way, and Ways, and a Way,
And the High Soul climbs the High Way,
And the Low Soul gropes the Low,
And in between, on the misty flats,
The rest drift to and fro.
But to every man there openeth
A High Way, and a Low,
And every man decideth
The Way his soul shall go.

How—When—Where

It is not so much *where* you live,
As *how*, and *why*, and *when* you live,
That answers in the affirmative,
Or maybe in the negative,
The question—Are you fit to live?

It is not so much *where* you live,
As *how* you live, and whether good
Flows from you through your neighbourhood.

And *why* you live, and whether you
Aim high and noblest ends pursue,
And keep Life brimming full and true.

And *when* you live, and whether Time
Is at its nadir or its prime,
And whether you descend or climb.

It is not so much *where* you live,
As whether while you live you *live*
And to the world your highest give,
And so make answer positive
That you are truly fit to live.

The Day—The Way

Not for one single day
Can I discern my way,
But this I surely know,—
Who gives the day,
Will show the way,
So I securely go.

New Year's Day—and Every Day

Each man is Captain of his Soul,
And each man his own Crew,
But the Pilot knows the Unknown Seas,
And He will bring us through.

We break new seas to-day,—
Our eager keels quest unaccustomed waters,
And, from the vast uncharted waste in front,
The mystic circles leap
To greet our prows with mightiest possibilities;
Bringing us—what?
    —Dread shoals and shifting banks?
    —And calms and storms?
    —And clouds and biting gales?
    —And wreck and loss?
    —And valiant fighting-times?
And, maybe, Death!—and so, the Larger Life!

For should the Pilot deem it best
To cut the voyage short,

He sees beyond the sky-line, and
He'll bring us into Port.

And, maybe, Life—Life on a bounding tide
　　And chance of glorious deeds;—
　　Of help swift-borne to drowning mariners;
　　Of cheer to ships dismasted in the gale;
　　Of succours given unasked and joyfully;
　　Of mighty service to all needy souls.

　　So—Ho for the Pilot's orders,
　　Whatever course He makes!
　　For He sees beyond the sky-line,
　　And He never makes mistakes.

And, maybe, Golden Days,
　　Full freighted with delight!
　　—And wide free seas of unimagined bliss,
　　—And Treasure Isles, and Kingdoms to be won,
　　—And Undiscovered Countries, and New Kin.

　　For each man captains his own Soul,
　　And chooses his own Crew,
　　But the Pilot knows the Unknown Seas,
　　And He will bring us through.

In Narrow Ways

Some lives are set in narrow ways,
By Love's wise tenderness.
They seem to suffer all their days
Life's direst storm and stress.
But God shall raise them up at length,
His purposes are sure,
He for their weakness shall give strength,
For every ill a cure.

God's Signpost

See there!—God's signpost, standing at the ways
Which every man of his free-will must go,—
Up the steep hill,—or down the winding ways,—
One or the other every man must go.

He forces no man, each must choose his way,
And as he chooses so the end will be,
One went in front to point the Perfect Way,
Who follows fears not where the end will be.

from The Cross at the Cross-ways

51

And Thou?

"For thee,—earth's fetters worn;
For thee,—the life forlorn;
For thee,—the crown of thorn;
For thee,—the death of scorn;
All this,—and that last agony,
I bore for thee.
What hast thou done for Me?"

Lord, to Thy name
I build a noble fane,
Chaste and replete
With all things fair and meet
Thy worship to maintain,
And dowered it complete
With every requisite.

"Thou hadst thy reward!"
Nay but,—Lord! . . . . Lord! . . . .
"Thou hadst thy reward!"

"And thou?"
Lord, I bring nought.
In humble ways I sought
To bring to dull gray days
Some gleam of light,
Some touch of grace,
Some lifting of the night.
I strove to teach Thy love,
But no success my work did bless.
Dear Lord, forgive my emptiness!

"Thou hast well done,
My faithful one.

I measure worth by effort, not success.
Not what thou didst, but what thy striving meant
Is my just gauge of thine accomplishment.
Come—enter in, and share my happiness!"

Freemen

Let no man stand between my God and me!
I claim a Free man's right
Of intercourse direct with Him,
Who gave me Freedom with the air and light.
God made me free.—
Let no man stand between
Me and my liberty!

We need no priest to tell us God is Love.—
Have we not eyes to see,
And minds to apprehend, and hearts
That leap responsive to His Charity?
God's gifts are free.—
Let no man stand between
Us and His liberty!

We need no priest to point a way to heaven.—
God's heaven is here,—is there,—
Man's birthright, with the light and air,—
"God is His own and best interpreter."
His ways are free.—
Let no man stand between
Us and His liberty!

Let no man strive to rob us of this right!
For this, from age to age,
Our fathers did a mighty warfare wage,
And, by God's help, we'll keep our heritage!
God says—"Be Free!"
And we,—
"No man shall stand between
Our sons and liberty!"

The Churches

Two, in the darkness, sought the Cross,
But in their blindness found it not;
This way and that, in dole and loss,
They sought the Cross, but found it not.

"This way!"—the one insistent cried;
"Nay, this!"—the other quick replied;
And each the other's hope denied.

"I tell you, my way is the right!"
"Nay then, you stumbler in the night,
My way alone leads to the light!"

"Perverse!—Go then your own wrong road!"
"I go!—for my way leads to God."
And each his own way brusquely strode.

And up above, upon The Tree,
Christ's wounds broke in fresh agony.

Follow Me!

Lord, I would follow, but—
First, I would see what means that wondrous call
That peals so sweetly through Life's rainbow hall,
That thrills my heart with quivering golden chords,
And fills my soul with joys seraphical.

Lord, I would follow, but—
First, I would leave things straight before I go,—
Collect my dues, and pay the debts I owe;
Lest when I'm gone, and none is here to tend,
Time's ruthless hand my garnering o'erthrow.

Lord, I would follow, but—
First, I would see the end of this high road
That stretches straight before me, fair and broad;
So clear the way I cannot go astray,
It surely leads me equally to God.

Lord, I would follow,—yea,
Follow I *will*,—but first so much there is
That claims me in life's vast emergencies,—
Wrongs to be righted, great things to be done;
Shall I neglect these vital urgencies?

Who answers Christ's insistent call
Must give himself, his life, his all,
Without one backward look.
Who sets his hand unto the plow,
And glances back with anxious brow,
His calling hath mistook.
Christ claims him wholly for His own;
He must be Christ's and Christ's alone.

Visions

Thank God for Vision of the brighter day,
That dawns at last beyond this rough red way!
New life is there for those who dare,—
A life that all these sufferings shall repay;—

A life set free from all the grosser things
That warped our souls and bound the Spirit's wings,—
An entrance fair to larger air,
And certitude of nobler prosperings.

Only have vision and bold enterprise!
No task too great for men of unsealed eyes;
The Future stands with outstretched hands,
Press on and claim its high supremacies!

The Goal and the Way

The future lies
With those whose eyes
Are wide to the necessities,
And wider still
With fervent will,
To all the possibilities.

Times big with fate
Our wills await,
If we be ripe to occupy;
If we be bold
To seize and hold
This new-born soul of liberty.

And every man
Not only can,
But *must* the great occasion seize.
Never again
Will he attain
Such wondrous opportunities.

Be strong! Be true!
Claim your soul's due!
Let no man rob you of the prize!
The goal is near,
The way is clear,
Who falters now shames God, and dies.

IV

Burden-Bearers

Burden-Bearers

Burden-bearers are we all,
Great and small.
Burden-sharers be ye all,
Great and small!
Where another shares the load,
To draw nearer God.
Yet there are burdens we can share with none,
Save God;
And paths remote where we must walk alone,
With God;
For lonely burden and for path apart—
Thank God!
If these but serve to bring the burdened heart
To God.

Lonely Brother

Art thou lonely, O my brother?
Share thy little with another!
Stretch a hand to one unfriended,
And thy loneliness is ended.
So both thou and he
Shall less lonely be.
And of thy one loneliness
Shall come two's great happiness.

A Little Word

I spoke a word,
And no one heard;
I wrote a word,
And no one cared,
Or seemed to heed;
But after half a score of years
It blossomed in a fragrant deed.

Preachers and teachers all are we,—
Sowers of seeds unconsciously.
Our hearers are beyond our ken,
Yet all we give may come again
With usury of joy or pain.
We never know
To what one little word may grow.
See to it then that all your seeds
Be such as bring forth noble deeds.

Wanted—A Man!

What we lack and sorely need,
For want of which we bleed, and bleed,
Is men of a more Godly breed.—
Honest men in highest places;
Men with single aims and faces;
Men whose nobler thought outpaces
Thought of self, or power, or pelf;—
Men whose axes need no grinding;
Men who are not always minding

First their own concerns, and blinding
Their souls' eyes to larger things.—
Men of wide and Godly vision;
Men of quick and wise decision;
Men who shrink not at derision;—
Men whose souls have wings.

Quoted in part

Motives

Motives are seeds,
From which at times spring deeds
Not equal to the soul's outreaching hope.
Strive for the stars!
Count nought well done but best!
Then, with brave patience, leave the rest
To Him who knows.
He'll judge you justly ere the record close.

Work

All labour gained new dignity
Since He who all creation made
Toiled with His hands for daily bread
Right manfully.

No work is commonplace, if all
Be done as unto Him alone;
Life's simplest toil to Him is known
Who knoweth all.

63

Each smallest common thing He makes
Serves Him with its minutest part;
Man only with his wandering heart
His way forsakes.

His service is life's highest joy,
It yields fair fruit a hundred fold.
Be this our prayer—"Not fame, nor gold,
But—Thine employ!"

Darkness and Light

There is darkness still, gross darkness, Lord,
On this fair earth of Thine.
There are prisoners still in the prison-house,
Where never a light doth shine.
There are doors still bolted against Thee,
There are faces set like a wall;
And over them all the Shadow of Death
Hangs like a pall.
> Do you hear the voices calling,
> Out there in the black of the night?
> Do you hear the sobs of the women
> Who are barred from the blessed light?
> And the children,—the little children,—
> Do you hear their pitiful cry?
> O brothers, we must seek them,
> Or there in the dark they die!

Spread the Light! Spread the Light!
Till earth's remotest bounds have heard
The glory of the Living Word;
Till those that see not have their sight;

Till all the fringes of the night
Are lifted, and the long-closed doors
Are wide for ever to the Light.
Spread—the—Light!

> *O then shall dawn the golden days,*
> *To which true hearts are pressing;*
> *When earth's discordant strains shall blend—*
> *The one true God confessing;*
> *When Christly thought and Christly deed*
> *Shall bind each heart and nation,*
> *In one Grand Brotherhood of Men,*
> *And one high consecration.*

Quoted in part

Bring Us the Light

I hear a clear voice calling, calling,
Calling out of the night,
O, you who live in the Light of Life,
     Bring us the Light!

We are bound in the chains of darkness,
Our eyes received no sight,
O, you who have never been bond or blind,
     Bring us the Light!

We live amid turmoil and horror,
Where might is the only right,
O, you to whom life is liberty,
     Bring us the Light!

65

We stand in the ashes of ruins,
We are ready to fight the fight,
O, you whose feet are firm on the Rock,
    Bring us the Light!

You cannot—you shall not forget us,
Out here in the darkest night,
We are drowning men, we are dying men,
    Bring, O, bring us the Light!

To Whom Shall the World Henceforth Belong?

To whom shall the world henceforth belong,
And who shall go up and possess it?

To the Great-Hearts—the Strong
Who will suffer no wrong,
And where they find evil redress it.

—To the Men of Bold Sight,
Whose souls, seized of Light,
Found a work to be done and have done it.

—To the Valiant who fought
For a soul-lifting thought,
Saw the fight to be won and have won it.

—To the Men of Great Mind
Set on lifting their kind,
Who, regardless of danger, will do it.

66

—To the Men of Goodwill,
Who would cure all Life's ill,
And whose passion for peace will ensue it.

—To the Men who will bear
Their full share of Life's care,
And will rest not till wrongs be all righted.

—To the Stalwarts who toil
'Mid the seas of turmoil,
Till the Haven of Safety be sighted.

—To the Men of Good Fame
Who everything claim—
This world and the next—in their Master's great name;—

—To these shall the world henceforth belong,
And they shall go up and possess it;
Overmuch, overlong, has the world suffered wrong,
We are here by God's help to redress it.

Where Are You Going, Great-Heart?

Where are you going, Great-Heart,
With your eager face and your fiery grace?—
Where are you going, Great-Heart?

"To fight a fight with all my might,
For Truth and Justice, God and Right,
To grace all Life with His fair Light."
Then God go with you, Great-Heart!

Where are you going, Great-Heart?
  "To beard the Devil in his den;
  To smite him with the strength of ten;
  To set at large the souls of men."
    Then God go with you, Great-Heart!

Where are you going, Great-Heart?
  "To end the rule of knavery;
  To break the yoke of slavery;
  To give the world delivery."
    Then God go with you, Great-Heart!

Where are you going, Great-Heart?
  "To hurl high-stationed evil down;
  To set the Cross above the crown;
  To spread abroad My King's renown."
    Then God go with you, Great-Heart!

Where are you going, Great-Heart?
  "To cleanse the earth of noisome things;
  To draw from life its poison-stings;
  To give free play to Freedom's wings."
    Then God go with you, Great-Heart!

Where are you going, Great-Heart?
  "To lift To-day above the Past;
  To make To-morrow sure and fast;
  To nail God's colours to the mast."
    Then God go with you, Great-Heart!

Where are you going, Great-Heart?
  "To break down old dividing-lines;
  To carry out My Lord's designs;
  To build again His broken shrines."
    Then God go with you, Great-Heart!

Where are you going, Great-Heart?
　　"To set all burdened peoples free;
　　To win for all God's liberty;
　　To 'stablish His Sweet Sovereignty."
　　　　God goeth with you, Great-Heart!

Livingstone

To lift the sombre fringes of the Night,
To open lands long darkened to the Light,
To heal grim wounds, to give the blind new sight,
　　Right mightily wrought he.
　　　　Forth to the fight he fared,
　　　　High things and great he dared,
　　　　He thought of all men but himself,
　　　　Himself he never spared.
　　　　He greatly loved—
　　　　He greatly lived—
　　　　And died right mightily.

Like Him he served, he walked life's troublous ways,
With heart undaunted, and with calm, high face,
And gemmed each day with deeds of sweetest grace;
　　Full lovingly wrought he.
　　　　Forth to the fight he fared,
　　　　High things and great he dared,
　　　　In His Master's might, to spread the Light,
　　　　Right lovingly wrought he.
　　　　He greatly loved—
　　　　He greatly lived—
　　　　And died right mightily.

Like him he served, he would not turn aside;
Nor home nor friends could his true heart divide;
He served his Master, and naught else beside,
    Right faithfully wrought he.
        Forth to the fight he fared,
        High things and great he dared,
        In His Master's might, to spread the Light,
        Right faithfully wrought he.
        He greatly loved—
        He greatly lived—
        And died right mightily.

He passed like light across the darkened land,
And dying, left behind him this command,
"The door is open! So let it ever stand!"
    Full mightily wrought he.
        Forth to the fight he fared,
        High things and great he dared,
        In His Master's might, to spread the Light,
        Right mightily wrought he.
        He greatly loved—
        He greatly lived—
        And died right mightily.

Kapiolani[1]

Where the great green combers break in thunder on the
    barrier reefs,—
Where, unceasing, sounds the mighty diapason of the
    deep,—
Ringed in bursts of wild wave-laughter, ringed in leagues of
    flying foam,—
Long lagoons of softest azure, curving beaches white as
    snow,
Lap in sweetness and in beauty all the isles of Owhyhee.

Land more lovely sun ne'er shone on than these isles of
    Owhyhee,
Spendthrift Nature's wild profusion fashioned them like
    fairy bowers;
Yet behind—below the sweetness,—underneath the passion-
    flowers,
Lurked grim deeds, and things of horror, grisly Deaths, and
    ceaseless Fears,
Fears and Deaths that walked in Darkness, grisly Deaths
    and ceaseless Fears.

On the slope of Mauna Loa, in the pit of Kilauea,
In the lake of molten lava, in the sea of living fire,
In the place of Ceaseless Burnings, in her home of Wrath
    and Terror,
Dwelt the dreadful goddess Pélé—Pélé of the Lake of Fire;
Pélé of the place of torment, Pélé of the Lake of Fire.

---

[1] Kapiolani—pronounced Kah-pee-o-lahny, with a slight accent on
the second syllable.
  Mauna Loa—Mona Lo-ah.
  Kilauea—Kil-o-ee-ah.
  Halé-Mau-Mau—Ha-lee-Mah-oo-Man-oo.

In the dim far-off beginnings, Pélé flung the island up
From the bottom of the ocean, from the darksome under-
world;
Built them for a house to dwell in, built them for herself
alone,
So she claimed them and their people, claimed them as her
very own,
And they feared her, and they worshipped—Pélé, the
Remorseless One.

But, at times, when she lay sleeping, underneath the lake
of fire,
They forgot to do her reverence, they forgot the Fiery One;
Then in wrath the goddess thundered from the Lake of
Ceaseless Burnings,
Flamed and thundered in her anger, till the very skies
were red,
Poured black ruin on the island, shook it to its rocky bed.

Then in fear the people trembled and bethought them of
their sins,
And the great high priest of Pélé came like Death down
Mauna Loa,
Came to soothe the awful goddess, came to choose the
sacrifice,
Chose the fairest youth or maiden, pointed with a deadly
finger,
Led them weeping up the mountain, victims to the Lake
of Fire.

On the snowy beach of coral, youths and maidens full of
laughter,
Flower-bedecked and full of laughter, sported gaily in
the sun;

Up above, the slender palm-trees swung and shivered in
  the trade-wind,
All around them flowers and spices,—red hibiscus, sweet
  pandanus,
And behind, the labouring mountain groaned and growled
  unceasingly.

> *"Sea and sunshine,*
>   *Care is moonshine,*
> *All our hearts are light with laughter.*
>   *We are free*
>   *As sun and sea,*
> *What care we for what comes after?"*

> *Bride.*
> *"Life was sweet before Love found her,*
> *In his faery bowers.*
> *Life is sweeter,*
> *And completer,*
> *Since he found her,*
> *There, and crowned her*
> *With his fadeless flowers."*

> *Bridegroom.*
> *"Love sought long before he found her,*
> *Ne'er was love like ours!*
> *Long he sought her,*
> *E'er he caught her.*
> *But he found her*
> *There, and bound her*
> *With his fadeless flowers."*

> *"Gaily sporting,*
>   *Pleasure courting,*
> *Nought know we of care or sorrow.*

We are free
As sun and sea,
What care we what comes to-morrow?"

Louder still and louder, Pélé roars within her lake of fire,
And the youths and maidens trembling look in fear up
Mauna Loa,
Dreading sight of that grim figure stalking down the
mountain side;
For when Pélé claims her victims none the summons may
avoid.
Pélé calls for whom she chooses—whom she chooses goes,
—and dies.

See! He comes! They start in terror. There, along the
mountain side,
Death comes stalking, slowly, surely,—*Pélé must be satisfied.*
Which among them will he summon, with his dreadful
pointing finger?
All their hearts become as water, all their faces blanch
with fear,
Deaths they suffer in the waiting, while dread Death draws
near.

Now he stands in dreadful menace, seeking with a baleful
eye
For the sweetest and the fairest—for the meetest sacrifice.
"Choose, O choose!"—they cry in terror; "choose your victim and be gone,
For we each die deaths while waiting, till dread Pélé's
choice be known!
Choose your victim, Priest of Pélé, choose your victim and
be gone!"

Slowly points the dreadful finger, marks the newly-wedded
bride;

74

All the rest, save one, fall from her, as the living from the
    dead.
From the first of time's beginnings Pélé ne'er has been
    gainsaid;
Pélé chooses whom she chooses, each and all the choice
    abide,
For the common good and safety,—*Pélé must be satisfied!*

Still the mountail reels and shudders, still the awful
    thunders peal,
Like a snake the ruthless finger holds them all in terror
    still;
One is there whose life is broken, parted from his chosen
    bride.
But the threatening finger, heedless of the lives it may
    divide,
Lights upon a tiny maiden,—*Pélé must be satisfied!*

Slow, the grim high-priest of Pélé turns to climb the
    mountain side;
Slow, the victims turn and follow,—*Pélé must be satisfied.*
And the rest shrink, dumb and helpless, daring not to
    lift an eye,
While above, the labouring mountain cracks and belches
    living fires,
Till the island reels and shudders at dread Pélé's agonies.

But a greater one than Pélé walked the mountain side
    that day;—
To them, climbing, dumb and dim-eyed—like a flash of
    heavenly flame,
Swift and bright as saving angel, fair Kapiolani came,
Swiftly as a saving angel, gleaming like a heavenly flame,
Thirsting like a sword for battle, fair Kapiolani came.,

Radiant with the faith of martyrs, all aglow with new-born
zeal,
Burning to release the people from the bondage and the
thrall,
From the deadly thrall of Pélé, from the ever-threatening
doom,
From the everlasting menace, from the awful lake of fire,
Like a bright avenging angel fair Kapiolani came!

"Hear me now, you priest of Pélé, and ye men of Owhyhee!
Hearken! ye who cringe and tremble, at the sound of
Kilauea,
Fearful of the wrath of Pélé, fearful of the lake of fire!—
Priest, I say there is no Pélé! Pélé is not—never was!
Pélé lives but in your legends—there is only one true God!"

"Cursèd, thrice accursèd, you who thus great Pélé do defy,
Here, upon her sacred mountain, of a surety you shall die!
Pélé, mighty Pélé, Vengeance! Strike her with thy dreadful
doom!
So let every scoffer perish!—Pélé! Pélé! Pélé! come!"
And Kapiolani answered—"Pélé! Pélé! Pélé! come!"

Loud the mountain roared and thundered; shuddered all
who heard and saw,
Dauntless stood Kapiolani, dauntless with her faithful few.
"Come!" she cried again. "Come, Pélé! Smite me with thy
dreadful doom!
I am waiting, mighty Pélé!—Pélé! Pélé! Pélé! come!"
And the mountain roared and thundered;—but the goddess
did not come.

"Hearken, Priest! You have deceived us. All your life has
been a lie.

Black your heart is, red your hands are, with the blood of
    those who die.
All these years you have misled us with your awful threats
    of doom.
Now it ends! I do defy you, and your goddess I defy.
Pélé, is not, never has been. All your worship is a lie.

I will climb your sacred mountain, I will dare your lake
    of fire.
I will eat your sacred berries. I will dare your goddess there,
There and then to wreak her vengeance, then and there to
    come in fire,
And with awful burnings end me, now and for eternity;
But if Pélé does not end me, then her worship ends this
    day."

Then the great high priest of Pélé turned to fiery Kilauea.
"Come!" he said, "the goddess calls you!"—and they
    climbed the mountain side,
Up the slopes of Mauna Loa, to the hell of Kilauea,
With the bright blue sky above them, with the blazing sun
    above them,
While the mountain shook beneath them, and its head was
    wrapped in fire.

Fearful, hopeful, all the people crept along the shaking
    path,
Hardly breathing at their daring, thus to brave dread Pélé's
    wrath,
Bending low lest she should see them, breathing soft lest
    she should hear,
Certain that Kapiolani would be sacrificed that day,
To the vengeance of the goddess, to the anger of Pélé.

77

"As little child
On mother's breast,
O rest, my heart,
Have rest!
Who rests on Him
Is surely blest.
So rest, my heart,
Have rest!

As warrior bold
His foes among,
Be strong, my heart,
Be strong!
Who rests on Him
Shall ne'er go wrong.
Be strong, my heart,
Be strong!"

Thus, Kapiolani, dauntless, singing softly as she went,
With a face as calm and fearless as a child on pleasure bent,
Climbed the side of Mauna Loa, to the dreadful lake of fire.
While the mountain shook and thundered, while the people
    blanched and shuddered,
Climbed to Halé-Mau-Mau,—to the dreadful lake of fire.

All the people waited trembling, stood afar off, pale and
    trembling,
While Kapiolani, fearless, climbed up to the lake of fire,
With the fiery glow all round her, with a heavenly light
    about her,
Shining with a radiance brighter than since time began
    had shone
From the Lake of Ceaseless Burnings, from the dreadful
    lake of fire.

"Here," she cried, "I pluck your berries, Pélé,—and I
give you none!
See! I eat your sacred berries, Pélé,—and I give you none!
Pélé, here I break your tabus! Come, with all your dreadful
fires!
Burn me, Pélé! I defy you!—Pélé! Pélé! Pélé! come!"
Come now, Pélé, or for ever own that you are overcome!

"Pélé comes not. Is she sleeping? Is she wandering to-day?
Is she busy with her burnings? Has the goddess nought
to say?
Hear me, friends!—There is no Pélé! One true God alone
there is.
His, this mountain! His, these burnings! You, and I, and
all things,—His!
Goodness, Mercy, Loving-Kindness, Life Eternal—all are
His!

"From this day, let no man tremble, when he feels the
mountain shake!
From this day, no man or maiden shall be killed for Pélé's
sake!
From this day, we break the thraldom of the dreadful lake
of fire.
From this day, we pass for ever from the scourge of Pélé's
rod.—
From this day, Thou, Lord Jehovah, be our one and only
God!"

India

A land of lights and shadows intervolved,
A land of blazing sun and blackest night,
A fortress armed, and guarded jealously,
With every portal barred against the Light.

A land in thrall to ancient mystic faiths,
A land of iron creeds and gruesome deeds,
A land of superstitions vast and grim,
And all the noisome growths that Darkness breeds.

Like sunny waves upon an iron-bound coast,
The Light beats up against the close-barred doors,
And seeks vain entrance, yet beats on and on,
In hopeful faith which all defeat ignores.

But—time shall come, when, like a swelling tide,
The Word shall leap the barriers, and The Light
Shall sweep the land; and Faith and Love and Hope
Shall win for Christ this stronghold of the night.

How Many, Lord, Have Died

How many, Lord, have died
To clear the cumbered ways,
To set the Closed Door wide,
To free the future days.

To set the Closed Door wide,
To give Thee entrance free,

Right willingly they died,
Right glad they live with Thee.

Right willingly they died,
Right joyfully they live,
For ever by Thy side,
Since Thou dost honour give

To all who died for Thee,
To clear the cumbered ways,
To give Thee entrance free,
To build the future days.

Praise be to God for all
The lives so greatly given!
No soul of all who met the Call
But lives with Thee in heaven.

from All Clear!

No East or West

In Christ there is no East or West,
  In Him no South or North,
But one great Fellowship of Love
  Throughout the whole wide earth.

In Him shall true hearts everywhere
  Their high communion find.
His service is the golden cord
  Close-binding all mankind.

Join hands then, Brothers of the Faith,
   Whate'er your race may be!—
Who serves my Father as a son
   Is surely kin to me.

In Christ now meet both East and West,
   In Him meet South and North,
All Christly souls are one in Him,
   Throughout the whole wide earth.

Break Down the Walls

Break down the old dividing walls
Of sect, and rivalry, and schism,
And heal the body of Thy Christ
With anoint of Thy chrism!

Let the strong wind of Thy sweet grace
Sweep through Thy cumbered house, and chase
The miasms from the Holy Place!

Let Thy white beam of light beat in,
And from each darkest corner win
The shadows that have sheltered sin!

Cleanse it of shibboleths and strife,
End all the discords that were rife,
Heal the old wounds and give new life!

Break down the hedges that have grown
So thickly all about Thy throne,

And clear the paths, that every soul
That seeks Thee—of himself alone
May find, and be made whole!—

One church, one all-harmonious voice,
One passion for Thy High Employs,
One heart of gold without alloys,
One striving for the higher joys,
One Christ, one Cross, one only Lord,
One living of the Living Word.

We Are All Kin

We are all kin—oh, make us kin indeed!
Spirit of Christ, we answer to Thy Call
Our Father makes of us one family
One Infinite Great Love doth claim us all,—
          All one in Him!

We are all kin, though wide our various ways.
Spirit of Christ, that lives within all life,
Break down the barriers that time has reared,
Heal every wound and end the fruitless strife!

Love Ever Gives

Love ever gives,—
Forgives—outlives,—
And ever stands
With open hands.
And, while it lives,
It gives.
For this is Love's prerogative,—
To give,—and give,—and give.

V

When He Tries the Hearts of Men

When He Tries the Hearts of Men

As gold is tried in the furnace,
So He tries the hearts of men;
And the dwale and the dross shall suffer loss,
When He tries the hearts of men.
And the wood, and the hay, and the stubble
Shall pass in the flame away,
For gain is loss, and loss is gain,
And treasure of earth is poor and vain,
When He tries the hearts of men.

As gold is refined in the furnace,
So He fines the hearts of men.
The purge of the flame doth rid them of shame,
When He tries the hearts of men.
O, better than gold, yea, than much fine gold,
When He tries the hearts of men,
Are Faith, and Hope, and Truth, and Love,
And the Wisdom that cometh from above,
When He tries the hearts of men.

Profit and Loss

Profit?—Loss?
Who shall declare this good—that ill?—
When good and ill so intertwine
But to fulfill the vast design
Of an Omniscient Will?—
When seeming gain but turns to loss,—
When earthly treasure proves but dross,—

And what seemed loss but turns again
To high, eternal gain?

Wisest the man who does his best,
And leaves the rest
To Him Who counts not deeds alone,
But sees the root, the flower, the fruit,
And calls them one.

The Two Men

Two men in me I find,
Of very different mind,—
    One strives at times for good,
    And one, in earthlier mood,
With lower things is strangely intertwined.

The one is not all ills,
The other grace reveals;
    But yet they are so mixed,
    My soul doth stand betwixt,
And neither one nor other all fulfills.

I can but take my stand,
And bear a lusty hand,—
    This one, my best to aid,
    And that, to embuscade,
And leave it all to You understand.

My Treasure

Treasure I sought
Over land and sea,
And dearly I bought
Prosperity.
But nought that I gained,
On land or sea,
Brought ever a lasting good to me.

Pleasure I sought
Over sea and land,
And snatched at life
With eager hånd.
But nought that I found,
On land or sea,
Brought ever a lasting joy to me,

For treasure of earth
Is fleeting gain,
And Pleasure is but
A mask for pain.
Life asketh more,
And ever stands,
With outstretched hands by an opening door.

And then at last,
My wanderings o'er,
All that I sought,
And God's good more,
Lay waiting for me
At my own door,—
Yea, more than I sought was at my door.

He let me scour
The world, to show
His Love and Power
Must all bestow.
All mine own strivings
Had brought me nought;
He gave me more than all I had sought.

Philosopher's Garden

"See this my garden,
Large and fair!"
—Thus, to his friend,
The Philosopher.

" 'Tis not too long,"
His friend replied,
With truth exact,—
"Nor yet too wide.
But well compact,
If somewhat cramped
On every side."

Quick the reply—
"But see how high!—
It reaches up
To God's blue sky!"

Not by their size
Measure we men
Or things.

Wisdom, with eyes
Washed in the fire,
Seeketh the things
That are higher—
Things that have wings,
Thoughts that aspire.

Debtor and Creditor Am I

All who have lived and gone,
             Since Time began,—
And all that they have ever done,
             Since Time began,—
Their every thought, and word, and deed,
Has been unconsciously a seed,
Bringing its influence to bear
Upon my mind and character.
Yea, each and all, in their degree,
Have had their part in making *me*,—
And *you*,—
Just simple you, and simple me.

And equally—

             Till Time shall end,
             And on through all eternity,—
In its degree,
Each thought and word and deed of mine,
Or makes or mars God's fair design.
Not one but has its due effect,
In ways by me all unsuspect,
On all who shall come after me.

No tiniest ripple on the sea
But tells on its immensity.

Here as I stand—a simple man—
I am Time's heir
                Since Time began.
And more,—in my degree, Progenitor
Of all that Time may have in store;—
Debtor and Creditor in one
Of all that has been, shall be, done.
I am at once effect and cause
Of all that is to be or was.
Enough, in truth, to make one pause
In awe-struck wonder at the laws
Which suffer no least thing to fail
In carrying on the wondrous tale.

In God's economy there is
No end to once-born energies.

The very leaf that falls and dies
Lives on again in other guise;
And no man for himself alone
Can live, or his account disown.
However small, for good or ill,
He doth Life's purposes fulfil,
And graves upon the deathless scroll
The endless record of his soul.
God's primal word was *"Let there be!"*
And therewith—Life's eternity.

Ceiled Houses
A Message for These Times

(Two thousand five hundred years ago Haggai delivered this message.
It has been on the way ever since, and is as much needed to-day as it
was then. Conditions alter. Facts and results unfortunately remain the
same. The world must bear its load until it learns its lesson.)

"What are these ceiled houses?"
Asked the Prophet coldly,—
His eyes like smouldering fires,
And the people answered boldly,—
"These be our houses, Man of God,
The houses where we dwell."

"And these half-builded walls?"
And they answered, timorous-boldly,—
"That is the Lord's house, waiting safer times
To finish building. . . .
We have had so much to do . . .
Our flocks to tend, our crops to rear,
Our wives and little ones to guard and cherish,
Our cities to repair,—
And all o'erburdenened with the care
Of foes against us everywhere."

Then flamed the God within him,—
"Is this a time to hap yourselves in comfort,
And the Lord's house still unbuilt?
Thus saith the Lord,—
  Consider now your ways!—
  Hard you have toiled and builded—for yourselves,
  Each man of you has toiled and builded—for himself;
  Early and late you toiled and builded—for yourselves,
  And yet you have not prospered.
  Much have you sown—and yet have little reaped,

93

Much have you eaten—but were hungry still,
Much drunk—yet were not filled,
Much clothing worn—but yet were never warm,
And that you earned you put in bags with holes.
You looked for much, and little came of it.—
And why?—
Because of this Mine House left desolate!
Hard have you toiled—but not for Me;—
Much have you cared—but not for Me;
And so—because you left Me out of it,
Lo, I have blown upon your work
And brought it all to nought.
Consider now your ways!"

Then did that people take God's word to heart
And turned again to Him;
And He abode with them and prospered them.

And unto us He says,—
"Ay, you have built to Me most wondrously,
But yet your hearts you turned away from Me,
And followed other gods.
And I have prospered you most bounteously,
But yet your hearts you turned away from Me,
And followed other gods.
Wealth, Pleasure, Power, Ease,—and baser things,—
These were your gods.
And so I blew upon your work
And brought it low.
For I, God, am a jealous God;
Yea, I am very jealous for your good.
Ye cannot serve these other gods and Me;
Consider now your ways!
And choose this day whom ye will serve.
Your self-made gods or Me!"

Judgment Day

Every day is Judgment Day,
Count on no to-morrow.
He who will not, when he may,
Act to-day, to-day, to-day,
Doth but borrow
Sorrow.

In Every Man

In every soul of all mankind
Somewhat of Christ I find,
          Somewhat of Christ—and thee;
For in each one there surely dwells
That something which most surely spells
          Life's immortality.

Beclouded oft, and oft obscure,
In peril oft of forfeiture,
And lost in many a plicature,
          Yet in each one there is
Such hope of soul-recoveries,
Such grace of soul-discoveries,
That in each life the seed there lies
          Of high immortal destinies.

And so, for love of Christ—and thee,
I will not cease to seek and find,
          In all mankind,
That hope of immortality
Which dwells so sacramentally
          In Christ—and thee.

95

Some Blessed

Blessed are they that have eyes to see.
  They shall find God everywhere.
  They shall see Him where others see stones.

Blessed are they that have understanding hearts.
  To them shall be multipled Kingdoms of Delight.

Blessed are they that see visions.
  They shall rejoice in the hidden ways of God.

Blessed are the song-ful of soul.
  They carry light and joy to shadowed lives.

Blessed are they who rejoice in the power of prayer.
  They draw very near to God.

Blessed are they who know the power of Love.
  They dwell in God, for God is Love.

Blessed are the faithful strong.
  They are the right hands of God.

Blessed are they that dwell in peace,—
  If they forget not God.

*Blessed are they who, through tribulation, have come to
    perfect trust in God.*
  Theirs is the peace which passeth understanding.

*Blessed are the burdened of heart to whom The Comforter
    has come.*
  They foretaste the joy of heaven.

Quoted in part

VI

The Call of the Dead

The Call of the Dead

Do you hear a deep voice calling?—
. Calling persistently?—
Like the sound of God's great waters,—
Calling insistently?
'Tis the voice of our dead, our myriad dead,
Calling to you and me;—

"By the red deaths we have suffered,
By the fiery paths we trod,
By the lives we gave All Life to save,—
We call you back to God.

"We call you from your trifling
With the petty things of life;
We cry aloud for a new world vowed
To a world-redeeming strife.

"We call you to cut the cankers
That have grown around your growth;
We call you from by-ways to High Ways,
And the pledge of a new God-troth.

"We call you to His high service;
You have followed other gods;
Their baneful ways brought the evil days,
And loosed the grim red floods.

"On your knees, on your knees, seek pardon
For the wrongs that have been done!—
For the perverse wills, and the active ills,
And the high things left undone!

"One way there is,—one only,
Whereby ye may stand sure;
One way by which ye may withstand
All foes, and Life's High Ways command,
And make your building sure.—
Take God once more as Cousellor
Work with Him, hand in hand,
Build surely, in His Grace and Power,
The nobler things that shall endure,
And, having done all,—STAND!"

For the Men at the Front

Lord God of Hosts, whose mighty hand
Dominion holds on sea and land,
In Peace and War Thy Will we see
Shaping the larger liberty.
      Nations may rise and nations fall,
      Thy Changeless Purpose rules them all.

When Death flies swift on wave or field,
Be Thou a sure defence and shield!
Console and succour those who fall,
And help and hearten each and all!
      O, hear a people's prayers for those
      Who fearless face their country's foes!

For those who weak and broken lie,
In weariness and agony—
Great Healer, to their beds of pain
Come, touch, and make them whole again!
      O, hear a people's prayers, and bless
      Thy servants in their hour of stress!

For those to whom the call shall come
We pray Thy tender welcome home.
The toil, the bitterness, all past,
We trust them to Thy Love at last.
      O, hear a people's prayers for all
      Who, nobly striving, nobly fall!

To every stricken heart and home,
O, come! In tenderest pity, come!
To anxious souls who wait in fear,
Be Thou most wonderfully near!
      And hear a people's prayers, for faith
      To quicken life and conquer death!

For those who minister and heal,
And spend themselves, their skill, their zeal—
Renew their hearts with Christ-like faith,
And guard them from disease and death.
      And in Thine own good time, Lord, send
      Thy Peace on earth till Time shall end!

The Builders

The City of God is within you,—
In every man its site,
Foundations all laid ready
For His Temple of Delight.
But who would build upon them
Must, like the men of old,
With the left hand grasp the sword,
With the right the trowel hold.

For foes are all around him,
Cunning, and fierce, and bold,
Ever seeking to confound him,
Or to buy his soul for gold.
If he would build securely,
And build him firm and broad,—
Like those ancient men
He must toil, and then,
If needs be, fight,
To uphold his right
To build his City of God.

The Goodly Company

Thou with us, and we with Thee,
Maketh goodly company,
Proof against all villainy,
Strong to vanquish tyranny;
Thou with us, and we with Thee,
Maketh goodly company.

Who would fight a goodly fight
Must have cause both just and right,
Then, with God's good oversight,
He in mail of proof is dight;
Who would fight a goodly fight
Must have cause both just and right.

Who would God upon his side,
And with Him would be allied,
By God's will his course must guide;

Fully then he's fortified,
Who hath God upon his side,
And with Him is close allied.

What Did You See Out There, My Lad?

What did you see out there, my lad,
That has set that look in your eyes?
You went out a boy, you have come back a man,
With strange new depths underneath your tan;
What was it you saw out there, my lad,
That set such deeps in your eyes?

"Strange things,—and sad,—and wonderful,—
Things that I scarce can tell,—
I have been in the sweep of the Reaper's scythe,—
With God,—and Christ,—and hell.

"I have seen Christ doing Christly deeds;
I have seen the devil at play;
I have grimped to the sod in the hand of God;
I have seen the godless pray.

"I have seen Death blast out suddenly
From a clear blue summer sky;
I have slain like Cain with a blazing brain:
I have heard the wounded cry.

"I have lain alone among the dead,
With no hope but to die;
I have seen them killing the wounded ones;
I have seen them crucify.

103

"I have seen the Devil in petticoats
Wiling the souls of men;
I have seen great sinners do great deeds
And turn to their sins again.

"I have sped through hells of fiery hail,
With fell red-fury shod;
I have heard the whisper of a Voice;
I have looked in the face of God."

You've a right to your deep, high look, my lad,
You have met God in the ways;
And no man looks into His face
But he feels it all his days.
You've a right to your deep, high look, my lad,
And we thank Him for His grace.

Sorrow Shall Make Us Kin

The Cark of Care has bitten in
To the core of every heart,
And the stress of life set lives apart,
In the toil and the moil and the grime of the mart,
But—

    —Sorrow shall make us kin.

Too much and too little have come between;
Too often, with jealous glance,
We have looked askance at the wayward chance
Which makes up the hazard of Circumstance;
But—

    —Sorrow shall make us kin.

104

Shoulder to shoulder, Life's life to win,
We have fought the evil powers,
Now sorrow is yours and sorrow is ours,
And over us all the black cloud lowers;
But—
                    —*Sorrow shall make us kin.*

One died on the Cross to vanquish sin,
In untold depth of woe,
By the Nail, and the Spear, and the Thorn, we
    know
He is kinsman now as long ago,
For—
                    -Sorrow hath made us kin.

The whole world groans in its anguish keen,
And the whole earth suffers dearth,
But Life is coming to nobler birth
Since man is discerning his fellows' worth,
For—
                    —*Sorrow hath made us kin.*

Hail!—and Farewell!

They died that we might live,—
Hail!—And Farewell!
—All honour give
To those who, nobly striving, nobly fell,
That we might live!

That we might live they died,—
Hail!—And Farewell!

105

—Their courage tried,
By every mean device of treacherous hate,
Like Kings they died.

Eternal honour give,—
Hail!—And Farewell!
—To those who died,
In that full splendour of heroic pride,
That we might live!

After the Storm

After the storm—Thy calm,—
After the earthquake, wind, and fire,—
The still, small voice,
Which yet doth pierce the marrow of our hearts
And makes our souls rejoice.

The whirlwind racked our Mounts of Selfish Ease;—
Thy Hand was in it, but we did not see.
The earthquake shook our proud-built buttresses;—
Thy Hand was in it, but we could not see.
The fire devoured our bravest and our best,—
Thy Hand was in it, but we would not see.
But now—Thy ways are manifest,
And, dimly, Lord, we see.

Wrapped in the mantle of our sorrows, now
Before Thee in the cavern's mouth we stand;
Behind us,—shall Thy mysteries of woe;
Before us,—visions of Thy Promised Land.

106

A land swept clean by earthquake, storm and fire,—
A land wherein Thy Spirit may rejoice,
Where Faith and Hope, with Love enthroned, conspire
To build Thy Kingdom of the still, small voice.

That still, small voice that yet proclaims Thy will,
Above the thunders of the battle-plain,
That bids man his high destiny fulfill,
And rise, and reap in full Thy golden grain.

Thou hast made chaos of our old content,
Purged us with fire, and winnowed us with woe;
We were forgetting that Thy gifts are meant
Only to wean us from the things below.

Yea, we forgot that all life's joys are sent,
Not as an end, but of Thy favour lent
For our poor natures' sweet encouragement,
And for our souls' most high ennoblement.

Help us to purge us of those lower things,
Which, growing, brought this world-catastrophe!
Help us to build, of these our sufferings,
Temples of Grace all dedicate to Thee!

Unless! Unless!

See now, my brothers,—
One and all
We met The Call
With hearts unbreakable,

And bore the brunt
Of woes unspeakable.
    But—on in front—
    Just on in front—
    Lie depths of horror and distress.
    Foul pits of utter ugliness.
    Of misery and wretchedness,
    Beyond the power of man to express,—
    Unless! . . . .
    . . . . Unless!—

One only way there is by which this load
Of coming ill may yet be turned to good,—
One—only—way,—
        Come back to God!

No laws, no cleverness, no statesmanship
Of man can save the world and with new life equip;
One Power alone,—*Come back to God,*
        And His allegiance own!

Cast out the evils that our souls debased!
Cleanse out Life's temple! Sweep it clean and chaste!
Let His fair image be no more defaced!—
        Come back to God!

Come back to God!—
The only road by which the coming ill
May yet be turned to good,—
        Come back to God!
           Come back to God!

Dies Irae—Dies Pacis

"Only through Me!" . . . The clear, high call comes pealing,
Above the thunders of the battle-plain;—
"Only through Me can Life's red wounds find healing;
Only through Me shall Earth have peace again.

Only through Me! . . . Love's Might, all might transcending,
Alone can draw the poison-fangs of Hate.
Yours the beginning!—Mine a nobler ending,—
Peace upon Earth, and Man regenerate!

Only through Me can come the great awakening;
Wrong cannot right the wrongs that Wrong hath done;
Only through Me, all other gods forsaking,
Can ye attain the heights that must be won.

Only through Me shall Victory be sounded;
Only through Me can Right wield righteous sword;
Only through Me shall Peace be surely founded;
Only through Me. . . . . *Then bid Me to the Board!*"

Can we not rise to such great height of glory?
Shall this vast sorrow spend itself in vain?
Shall future ages tell the woeful story,—
"Christ by His own was crucified again?"

The Tests of Peace

No less than War Peace has its acid tests.

War is most dreadful hell;
And yet full well
May Peace be fouler than War's foulest hell,
Unless some strong new soul of life
Rise up to stay,—
To stay if need be with the knife,
The slow, insidious dry-rot of decay,
Which no whit less than war doth Christ betray,—
—Rise up to charge all life with quickened zest
For things not only better but *the best*.

Peace that means laxing of the soul's upreach,—
Peace that means but an ever-widening breach
              'Twixt man and man,—and so
              'Twixt man and God,—
Peace that means tolerance of obvious wrong,—
Peace that means safety only for the strong,—
Peace that means heedlessness of others' woes,—
Peace that means chance new burdens to impose,—
Peace that means wealth outsweated from the poor,—
Peace that means Greed's perfidious coverture,—
Peace that means palaces on pigstyes reared,—
Peace that means gold with brave men's blood be-
      smeared,—
Peace that means virtue offered out for hire,—
Peace that means honour trampled in the mire, —
Peace that means ill-division of life's good,—
Peace that means ill-adjustment of life's load,—
Peace that means brimming bowls and ruined lives,—
Peace that for sake of gain at shame connives,—
Peace that maintains the standards of the past,—

Peace that still leaves the Lord of All outcast,—
That is no peace!—
A mocking parody of peace,—
            It shall not last.

Peace without God as base and cornerstone,—
Peace without Right concreted in its frame,—
Peace without Truth up-pillaring its dome,—
Peace without Justice buttressing its walls,—
Peace without Grace as its fair furnishing,—
Peace without Honour as its golden lamp,—
Peace that is all unfortified with Love,—
That is no peace,—a straw house built on sand,
Which life's new needs can never meet
Nor time's rough circumstance withstand.
Get back to God and Fundamental Right!
Build His New House with patience infinite!
Resolve Life's vast complexities to ways
More simple, and exalt the days!
Let all Life's warp and woof be interwove
With gold of noble thought and radiant love,
So—only so—shall Life's New Temple stand,
Rock-firm, unshakable, His rightful deodand.

See to it then, Ye Builders of the Peace,
And build with bold emprise Life's new-won liberties!
Build His fair kingdom as He first designed
To His unending glory
And the welfare of mankind!

                                from And After?

111

The Vision Splendid

Here—or hereafter—you shall see it ended,
This mighty work to which your souls are set;
If from beyond—then, with the vision splendid,
You shall smile back and never know regret.

Be this your vision!—through you, Life transfigured,
Uplift, redeemed from its forlorn estate,
Purged of the stains which once its soul disfigured,
Healed and restored, and wholly consecrate.

Christ's own rich blood, for healing of the nations,
Poured through His heart the message of reprieve;
God's holy martyrs built on His foundations,
Built with their lives and died that Life might live.

Now, in their train, your blood shall bring like healing;
You, like the saints, have freely given your all,
And your high deaths, God's purposes revealing,
Sound through the earth His mighty Clarion Call.

O, not in vain has been your great endeavour;
For, by your dyings, Life is born again,
And greater love hath no man tokened ever,
Than with his life to purchase Life's high gain.

Peace

Peace in our time, O Lord,
To all the peoples—Peace!
Peace surely based upon Thy Will
And built in righteousness.

Thy power alone can break
The fetters that enchain
The sorely-stricken soul of life,
And make it live again.

Too long mistrust and fear
Have held our souls in thrall;
Sweep through the earth, keen breath of heaven,
And sound a nobler call!
 Come, as Thou didst of old,
 In love so great that men
 Shall cast aside all other gods
 And turn to Thee again!

O, shall we never learn
The truth all time has taught,—
That without God as architect
Our building comes to naught?
 Lord, help us, and inspire
 Our hearts and lives, that we
 May build, with all Thy wondrous gifts,
 A Kingdom meet for Thee!

Peace in our time, O Lord,
To all the peoples—Peace!
Peace that shall crown a glad new world,
With Thy High Sovereignties.

 O Living Christ, who still
 Dost all our burdens share,
 Come now and reign within the hearts
 Of all men everywhere!

Out of Darkness, Light

From this dread sowing, grant us harvest, Lord,
Of Nobler Doing, and of Loftier Hope,—
An All-Embracing and Enduring Peace,—
A Bond of States, a Pact of Peoples, based
On no caprice of royal whim, but on
Foundation mightier than the mightiest throne—
The Well-Considered Will of All the Lands.
Therewith,—a simpler, purer, larger life,
Unhampered by the dread of war's alarms,
A life attuned to closer touch with Thee,
And golden-threaded with Thy Charity;—
A Sweeter Earth,—a Nearer Heaven,—a World
As emulous in Peace as once in War,
And striving ever upward towards The Goal.

> *So, once again, through Death shall come New
> Life,*
> *And out of Darkness, Light.*

from Policeman X

Why?

With what intent
Was this grim sorrow sent?—
What meaning lies in such dread sacrifice?
Of a surety it is meant
To teach us this,—
That man, however fallen, still may rise

114

If he repent,
Through sacrifice
To sacrament.
But—till he thereunto attain,
All sacrifice is made in vain.
Forced sacrifice no virtue wins,
Nor healeth any of his sins.

Free Men of God

Free men of God, the New Day breaks
In golden gleams across the sky;
The darkness of the night is past,
This is the Day of Victory.
    For this our fathers strove,
    In stern and fiery love—
    That men to come should be
    Born into liberty—
That all should be—as we are—Free!

Free men of God, gird up your loins,
And brace you for the final fight!
Strike home, strike home for Truth and Right!
—Yet bear yourselves as in His sight!
    For this our fathers fought,
    This with their lives they bought—
    That you and I should be
    Heirs of their liberty—
That all should be—as we are—Free!

Free men we are and so will be;
We claim free access unto Him,

Who widened all the bounds of life,
And us from bondage did redeem.
    Let no man intervene,
    Or draw a veil between
    Us and our God, for He
    Would have His people free,—
And we would be—as Thou art—Free.

Free men of God, your Birthright claim!
Our fathers won it with a price.
They paid in full to axe and flame,
Nor counted up the sacrifice.
    This is our heritage,
    And here we do engage,
    Each man unto his son
    Intact to pass it on.
So shall they be—as we are—Free!

Our Sure Defence, in times of stress,
Thy gates stand open, wide and free,
When men provoke and wrongs oppress,
We seek Thy wider liberty.
    With loftier mind and heart,
    Let each man bear his part!
    So—to the final fight,
    And God defend the right!
We shall, we must, we will be—Free!

VII

The Sacraments

The Sacrament of Love

Love is the sacrament of sacraments;
For God is Love, and Love is God;
Who loves knows Him, and in Him all the heights
And depths of those high rapturous delights
Which for Love's soul are very soul of life,
And through the troubled ways,—through stress and strife,
Bear the soul upward to that final goal
Where Life and Love make one full-rounded whole.

Love tints the grayest life with rose;
Love kindles fires 'mid winter snows.

Love draws the fallen from his sin;
Love helps the sinner grace to win.

Love lifts the fringes of the night;
Love gifts the eyes of Faith with sight.

Love to all loveliness is kin;
Love moulds all Life,—without,—within.

Love is the mightiest power on earth;
Love to Eternal Hope gives birth.

Love—the Beginning and the End—
All life and death doth comprehend.

Love lived in Death upon the Tree;
Love lives again, for you and me.

Love through eternity endures,
For God is Love,
And Love is God.
Thank God for Love,—His first,—then yours!

The Sacrament of Fire

Kneel always when you light a fire!
Kneel reverently, and thankful be
For God's unfailing charity,
And on the ascending flame inspire
A little prayer, that shall upbear
The incense of your thankfulness
For this sweet grace
Of warmth and light!
For here again is sacrifice
For your delight.

Within the wood,
That lived a joyous life
Through sunny days and rainy days
And winter storms and strife;—
Within the peat,
That drank the moorland sweet
Of bracken, whin, and sweet bell-heather,
And all the joy of gold gorse feather
Flaming like Love in wintriest weather,—
While snug below, in sun and snow,
Peat heard the beat of the padding feet
Of foal and dam, and ewe and lamb,
And the stamp of old bell-wether;—
Within the coal,
Where forests lie entombed,
Oak, elm, and chestnut, beech, and red pine bole,—
God shrined His sunshine, and enwombed
For you these stores of light and heat,
Your life-joys to complete.
These all have died that you might live;
Yours now the high prerogative
To loose their long captivities,—

To give them new sweet span of life
And fresh activities.

Kneel always when you light a fire!
Kneel reverently,
And grateful be
To God for His unfailing charity!

The Sacrament of Light

In that far-off dim dawn,
When chaos reigned, and earth was still
A formless void in darkness dight,
The Spirit, brooding o'er the deep,
Awoke Creation from its sleep
With that High Call—
"Let—There—Be—Light!"
And instant from the womb of night
Sprang forth the mystic seven-fold beam,
Ablaze with splendours bright.
God, in His Wisdom all supreme,
As His first act made—Light.

So, unto Him give praise!
Praise without ceasing!—Praise!—
That in His Wisdom Infinite,
When making Man for His delight,
Before He dowered him with sight,
He filled the world with radiance bright,
Lest, dulled with fear and void of hope,
With stumbling footsteps he should grope,
Through an eternal night.

121

To God eternal praise!
Praise without ceasing!—Praise!—
That in His Goodness Infinite
He blessed the world with Light.
Subserve it to His high employ,
And see thou use it right!

The Sacrament of Water

Crystal clear from the throne of God
Flows The River, The Shining River,
For ever full, for ever free,
It floweth everlastingly
Through the banks of Time to the Boundless Sea
Of Love indwelling Eternity.

Praise to God in running water,
Gleaming, glancing, running water!
Crystal clear its joyous cheer,
Dreaming, dancing, running water;
Amber-bright all slashed with white,
Sweet, romancing, running water;
Give God praise for all fair water!
His sweet grace is running water.

God's sweet grace is running water,
All fair, sparkling, running water,
Bubbling spring from rock or sod,—
Goodly thing,—the gift of God,—
Babbling praises as it flows,
Gathering graces as it grows,
Scattering joys where'er it goes;—
Praise to God in running water!

Blithely o'er its shallows purling,
Lithely through its narrows swirling,
Round its mossy boulders curling,
Glooming, gleaming, spooming, creaming
With new life so richly teeming
For the thirsty earth's redeeming;—
Give God praise for running water,
For all fair, fresh, running water!

The Sacrament of Food

Each meal should be a sacramental feast,—
A Eucharist each breaking of the bread,
Wherein we meet again our Great High Priest,
And pledge new troth to our exalted Head.

For all we eat doth come of sacrifice,—
Life out of Death,—since all we eat must yield
Life for our living,—and yet, nothing dies,
But in its giving finds its life fulfilled.

The wheat, the plant, the beast, and man, all give,
Each of their best, God's purpose to maintain,
And all subserve the end for which all live,
And pass,—to live more worthily again.

The Sacrament of Work

Upon thy bended knees thank God for work,—
Work—once man's penance, now his high reward!
For work to do and strength to do the work,
               We thank Thee, Lord!

Since outcast Adam toiled to make a home,
The primal curse a blessing has become,
Man in his toil finds recompense for loss,
A workless world had known nor Christ nor Cross.

Some toil for love, and some for simple greed,
Some reap a harvest past their utmost need,
More, in their less find truer happiness,
And all, in work, relief from bitterness.

A toiler with His hands was God's own Son;
Like His, to Him be all thy work well done.
None so forlorn as he that hath no work,
None so abject as he that work doth shirk.

Upon thy bended knees, thank God for work!
In workless days all ills and evils lurk;
For work to do, and strength to do the work,
               We thank Thee, Lord!

The Sacrament of Sleep

Thank God for sleep!
And, when you cannot sleep,
Still thank Him that you live
To lie awake.
And pray Him, of His grace,
When He sees fit, sweet sleep to give,
That you may rise, with new-born eyes,
To look once more into His shining face.

In sleep,—limbs all loose-laxed and slipt the chains—
We draw sweet-close to Him from whom our breath
Has life. In His sole hands we leave the reins,
In fullest faith trust Him for life or death.

This sleep in life close kinsman is to death;
And, as from sleep we wake to greet the day,
So, too, from death we shall with joy awake
To greet the glories of the Great Essay.

To His belov'd new life in sleep He gives,
And, unto all, awakening from sleep.
Each day is resurrection,—a new birth
To nearer heaven and re-created earth,—
To all Life's possibilities—of good
Or ill,—with joys and woes endued,—
Till that last, shortest sleep of all,
And that first great awakening from Life's thrall.

Thank God for sleep!
And, when you cannot sleep,
Still thank Him for the grace
That lets you live
To feel the comfort of His soft embrace.

The Sacrament of Sleep

Thank God for sleep!
And, when you cannot sleep,
Still thank Him that you live
To lie awake.
And pray Him, of His grace,
When He sees fit, sweet sleep to give,
That you may rise, with new-born eyes,
To look once more into His shining face.

In sleep,—limbs all loose-laxed and slipt the chains—
We draw sweet-close to Him from whom our breath
Has life. In His sole hands we leave the reins,
In fullest faith trust Him for life or death.

This sleep in life close kinsman is to death;
And, as from sleep we wake to greet the day,
So, too, from death we shall with joy awake
To greet the glories of the Great Essay.

To His belov'd new life in sleep He gives,
And, unto all, awakening from sleep.
Each day is resurrection,—a new birth
To nearer heaven and re-created earth,—
To all Life's possibilities—of good
Or ill,—with joys and woes endued,—
Till that last, shortest sleep of all,
And that first great awakening from Life's thrall.

Thank God for sleep!
And, when you cannot sleep,
Still thank Him for the grace
That lets you live
To feel the comfort of His soft embrace.

And suffers still, and will till knowledge grow.
But, by the pangs that for mankind He bore,
He showed The Way, and, going on before,
He made of Death the Opener of Life's Door.

The Sacrament of Life and Death

Life is God's sacramental gift
To man for his emprising,—
The talent given into his care
For his soul's exercising,—
A sacred trust bestowed on him
For his immortalising.

And He Who lends will one day ask
His own again with interest,—
See to it then, lest thou be found
Of those who failed Him in the test.

His equal gift is Death,—
Death, the Bead-Roller of all noble souls
Whose lives were given to questing noblest goals
Death is no foe, but Everyman's best friend;
Death is Life's true beginning, not its end;
Death is the Opener of the Golden Door
To that high Life which goes from more to more.
Dear Brother Death, who brings us sweet release
From all earth's sorrows with God's gift of Peace!

VIII

Sanctuary

Sanctuary

'Mid all the traffic of the ways,—
Turmoils without, within,—
Make in my heart a quiet place,
And come and dwell therein!

—A little shrine of quietness,
All sacred to Thyself,
Where Thou shalt all my soul possess,
And I may find myself;

—A little shelter from Life's stress,
Where I may lay me prone,
And bare my soul in lowliness,
And know as I am known;

—A solitude where I can think,
A haven of retreat,
Where of Thy Red Wine I may drink,
And of Thy White Bread eat;

—A little silent, sacred place,
Where we may commune hold;
Where Thy White Love shall me embrace
And from the world enfold;

—A little place of mystic grace,
Of self and sin swept bare,
Where I may look into Thy face,
And talk with Thee in prayer.

Come!—occupy my silent place,
And make Thy dwelling there!
More grace is wrought in quietness
Than any is aware.

The Secret Place

Each soul has its own secret place,
Where none may enter in,
Save it and God,—to them alone
What goeth on therein is known,—
To it and God alone.

And well for it if God be there,
And in supreme control;
For every deed comes of a seed,
And lonely seed may evil breed
In any lonely soul.

But none, except of his own will,
Need ever lonely be;
If he but quest, his Royal Guest
Will quick provide him with the best
Of all good Company.

In Time of Need

Better than I,
Thou knowest, Lord,
All my necessity,
And with a word
Thou canst it all supply.
Help other is there none
Save Thee alone;
Without Thee I'm undone.
And so, to Thee I cry,—

O, be Thou nigh!
For, better far than I,
Thou knowest, Lord,
All my necessity.

De Profundis

Out of the depths
To Thee, O Lord, I cried,
And Thou my pressing need
Hast ne'er denied.

Thy hand reached down,
The strong right hand of Love,
And lifted me right up
My cares above.

Had I not been
Sunk in the depths of woe,
I ne'er had known how much
To Thee I owe.

And so, although
The depths were very sore,
Through them I know Thee more
Than e'er before.

Out of the depths
My soul can rise to God,
Since He who died for me
This same way trod.

So, for the depths
I still will grateful be,
Since they made known to me
Thy Charity.

Prayer

'Tis not the length of time we stay,
Nor the multitudinous things we say,
But the heartiness with which we pray,
 That counts with Him who hears us.

Better one sigh and an upward glance,
A kindling of inward penitence,
Than years of loftiest pretence,
 To the heart of Him who bears us.

The Golden Cord

Through every minute of this day,
 Be with me, Lord!
Through every day of all this week,
 Be with me, Lord!
Through every week of all this year,
 Be with me, Lord!
Through all the years of all this life,
 Be with me, Lord!
So shall the days and weeks and years
Be threaded on a golden cord,

And all draw on with sweet accord
Unto Thy fulness, Lord,
That so, when time is past,
By grace, I may at last,
    Be with Thee, Lord.

Whirring Wheels

Lord, when on my bed I lie,
Sleepless, unto Thee I'll cry;
When my brain works overmuch,
Stay the wheels with Thy soft touch.

Just a quiet thought of Thee,
And of Thy sweet charity,—
Just a little prayer, and then
I will turn to sleep again.

Faith

Lord, give me faith!—to live from day to day,
With tranquil heart to do my simple part,
And, with my hand in Thine, just go Thy way.

Lord, give me faith!—to trust, if not to know;
With quiet mind in all things Thee to find,
And, child-like, go where Thou wouldst have me go.

Lord, give me faith!—to leave it all to Thee,
The future is Thy gift, I would not lift
The veil Thy Love has hung 'twixt it and me.

We Thank Thee, Lord

We thank thee, Lord,
That of Thy tender grace,
In our distress
Thou hast not left us wholly comfortless.

We thank Thee, Lord,
That of Thy wondrous might,
Into our night
Thou hast sent down the glory of the Light.

We thank Thee, Lord,
That all Thy wondrous ways,
Through all our days,
Are Wisdom, Right, and Ceaseless Tenderness.

A Father's Prayer

Lord, give me faith
As these have faith in me!
And Hope,
That springs eternally!
And Love,
Revealing Thee!
All else I leave
To Thy wide charity.

The Children

The children, Lord, the children!—
Not for ourselves we pray,
But for these little ones, whose feet
Are tender to the way.

For we have learned our lessons
Of Love, and Hope, and Trust;
But they have still to learn them,
'Mid the turmoil and the dust.

Thy hand was always stretched, Lord,
To lift us when we fell;
We leave them to thy Father-love
That doeth all things well.

When the wind and the rain beat on them,
O hap them in Thy breast,
When their feet grow worn with ways forlorn
Lift them up and give them rest.

137

High on Thy breast, Lord, bear them,
Above the flints and mire.
The way is long, the wind is strong,
But Love's arms never tire.

We have no wealth to leave them,
They must tread the paths we trod;
But all is well if but they dwell
In the Fatherhood of God.

And whatever else they learn, Lord,
May they learn this first of all,—
That the great heart of their Father
Will answer every call.

Per Ardua ad Astra

Lift me, O God, above myself,—
Above my highest spheres,
Above the thralling things of sense
To clearer atmospheres.

Lift me above the little things,—
My poor sufficiencies,
My perverse will, my lack of zeal,
My inefficiencies;—

Above the earth-born need that gropes,
With foolish hankerings,
About earth's cumbered lower slopes
For earthly garnerings.

Above the vanities and cates
Of the Forbidden Land;—
Above the passions and the hates
That flame there hand in hand.

Lift me, O God, above myself,
Above these lesser things,
Above my little gods of clay,
And all their capturings.

And grant my soul a glad new birth,
And fledge it strong new wings,
That it may soar above the earth
To nobler prosperings.

Lift me, O God, above myself,
That, in Thy time and day,
I somewhat grace Thy fosterings
And climb Thy loftier Way.

Thy Kingdom Come!

Thy Kingdom come!
And quickly, Lord!
For Life is a tempestuous sea,
Where storm-winds beat unceasingly
And drive us oft away from Thee.
        So, day by day,
        We ever pray—
        "Thy Kingdom come!
        Thy Kingdom come!"

Thy Kingdom come!
Lord, till it comes,
We are but voyagers who roam
With straining eyes amid the gloom,
And seek but cannot find our home.
                    So, day by day,
                    In faith we pray—
                    "Thy Kingdom come!
                    Thy Kingdom come!"

Thy Kingdom come!
For when it comes
Earth's crying wrongs will be redressed,
And man will make his chiefest quest
The Peace of God which giveth rest.
                    So, day by day,
                    In hope we pray—
                    "Thy Kingdom come!
                    Thy Kingdom come!"

Thy Kingdom come!
Ah, grant us, Lord,
To see the day when Thou shalt reign
Supreme within the hearts of men,
And Love shall dwell on earth again!
                    For that, Thy Day,
                    We ever pray—
                    "Thy Kingdom come!
                    Thy Kingdom come!"

Thy Will Be Done!

Thy Will be done!
Lord, when it is,
Earth will forsake her miseries
And turn again to Thee, where is
Sure hope of full recoveries.
         So, day by day,
         In faith we pray,—
         "Thy Will be done!
         Thy Will be done!"

Thy Will be done!
Until it is,
Life cannot know the untold bliss
Of full and free and sure release
From all that now doth mar its peace.
         So, day by day,
         In hope we pray—
         "Thy Will be done!
         Thy Will be done!"

Thy Will be done!
For Thy Will is
Man's deepest, highest, fullest joy,
Love's purest gold without alloy!
With thought of that our hearts we buoy,
         And, day by day,
         Full-faithed, we pray—
         "Thy Will be done!
         Thy Will be done!"

Thy Will be done!
Thy good will is
For every man such happiness,

Such freedom from life's care and stress,
As never man did yet possess;—
            And so each day
            With joy we pray—
            "Thy Will be done!
            Thy Will be done!"

Petition

O grant me this,—
In all my work,
Lord, of Thy best!—
High thought in true word drest,
To cheer, to lift,—
To comfort the depressed,—
To lighten darkness,—
To bring rest
To souls distrest.
In all my work, O manifest
Thy Will!
So shall the work be blest.

Liberty, Equality, Fraternity

O God, within whose sight
All men have equal right
   To worship Thee,
Break every bar that holds
Thy flock in diverse folds!
Thy Will from none withholds
   Full liberty.

Lord, set Thy Churches free
From foolish rivalry!
   Lord, set us free!
Let all past bitterness
Now and for ever cease,
And all our souls possess
   Thy charity!

Lord, set the people free!
Let all men draw to Thee
   In unity!
Thy temple courts are wide,
Therein let all abide
In peace, and side by side,
   Serve only Thee!

God, grant us now Thy peace!
Bid all dissensions cease!
   God, send us peace!
Peace in True Liberty,
Peace in Equality,
Peace and Fraternity,
   God, send us peace!

A New Earth

God grant us wisdom in these coming days,
And eyes unsealed, that we clear visions see
Of that new world that He would have us build,
To Life's ennoblement and His high ministry.

God give us sense,—God-sense of Life's new needs,
And souls aflame with new-born chivalries—
To cope with those black growths that foul the ways,—
To cleanse our poisoned founts with God-born energies.

To pledge our souls to nobler, loftier life,
To win the world to His fair sanctities,
To bind the nations in a Pact of Peace,
And free the Soul of Life for finer loyalties.

Not since Christ died upon His lonely cross
Has Time such prospect held of Life's new birth;
Not since the world of chaos first was born
Has man so clearly visaged hope of a new earth.

Not of our own might can we hope to rise
Above the ruts and soilures of the past,
But, with His help who did the first earth build,
With hearts courageous we may fairer build this last.

IX

Te Deum

A *Little Te Deum of the Commonplace*
A Fragment

With hearts responsive
And enfranchised eyes,
We thank Thee, Lord,—
For all things beautiful, and good, and true;
For things that seemed not good yet turned to good;
For all the sweet compulsions of Thy will
That chased, and tried, and wrought us to Thy shape;
For things unnumbered that we take of right,
And value first when first they are withheld;
For light and air; sweet sense of sound and smell;
For ears to hear the heavenly harmonies;
For eyes to see the unseen in the seen;
For vision of The Worker in the work;
For hearts to apprehend Thee everywhere;
                    We thank Thee, Lord!

For all the wonders of this wondrous world;—
The pure pearl splendours of the coming day,
The breaking east,—the rosy flush,—the Dawn,—
For that bright gem in morning's coronal,
That one lone star that gleams above the glow;
For that high glory of the impartial sun,—
The golden noonings big with promised life;
The matchless pageant of the evening skies,
The wide-flung gates,—the gleams of Paradise,—
Supremest visions of Thine artistry;
The sweet, soft gloaming, and the friendly stars;
The vesper stillness, and the creeping shades;
The moon's pale majesty; the pulsing dome,
Wherein we feel Thy great heart throbbing near;
For sweet laborious days and restful nights;
For work to do, and strength to do the work;
                    We thank Thee, Lord!

147

For those first tiny, prayerful-folded hands
That pierce the winter's crust, and softly bring
Life out of death, the endless mystery;—
For all the first sweet flushings of the Spring;
The greening earth, the tender heavenly blue;
The rich brown furrows gaping for the seed;
For all Thy grace in bursting bud and leaf,—
The bridal sweetness of the orchard trees,
Rose-tender in their coming fruitfulness;
The fragrant snow-drifts flung upon the breeze;
The grace and glory of the fruitless flowers,
Ambrosial beauty their reward and ours;
For hedgerows sweet with hawthorn and wild rose;
For meadows spread with gold and gemmed with stars;
For every tint of every tiniest flower;
For every daisy smiling to the sun;
For every bird that builds in joyous hope;
For every lamb that frisks beside its dam;
For every leaf that rustles in the wind;
For spiring poplar, and for spreading oak;
For queenly birch, and lofty swaying elm;
For the great cedar's benedictory grace;
For earth's ten thousand fragrant incenses,—
Sweet altar-gifts from leaf and fruit and flower;
For every wondrous thing that greens and grows;
For wide-spread cornlands,—billowing golden seas;
For rippling stream, and white-laced waterfall;
For purpling mountains; lakes like silver shields;
For white-piled clouds that float against the blue;
For tender green of far-off upland slopes;
For fringing forests and far-gleaming spires;
For those white peaks, serene and grand and still;
For that deep sea—a shallow to Thy love;
For round green hills, earth's full benignant breasts;
For sun-chased shadows flitting o'er the plain;

For gleam and gloom; for all life's counter-change;
For hope that quickens under darkening skies;
For all we see; for all that underlies,—
                            We thank Thee, Lord!

For that sweet impulse of the coming Spring,
For ripening Summer, and the harvesting;
For all the rich Autumnal glories spread,—
The flaming pageant of the ripening woods;
The fiery gorse, the heather-purpled hills;
The rustling leaves that fly before the wind,
And lie below the hedgerows whispering;
For meadows silver-white with hoary dew;
For sheer delight of tasting once again
That first crisp breath of winter in the air;
The pictured pane; the new white world without;
The sparkling hedgerow's witchery of lace;
The soft white flakes that fold the sleeping earth;
The cold without, the cheerier warmth within;
For red-heart roses in the winter snows;
For all the flower and fruit of Christmas-tide;
For all the glowing heart of Christmas-tide;
                            We thank Thee, Lord!

For all Thy ministries,—
For morning mist, and gently-falling dew;
For summer rains, for winter ice and snow;
For whispering wind and purifying storm;
For the reft clouds that show the tender blue;
For the forked flash and long tumultuous roll;
For mighty rains that wash the dim earth clean;
For the sweet promise of the seven-fold bow;
For the soft sunshine, and the still calm night;
For dimpled laughter of soft summer seas;
For latticed splendour of the sea-borne moon;

149

For gleaming sands, and granite-frontled cliffs;
For flying spume, and waves that whip the skies;
For rushing gale, and for the great glad calm;
For Might so mighty, and for Love so true,
With equal mind,

We thank Thee, Lord!

For maiden sweetness, and for strength of men;
For love's pure madness and its high estate;
For parentage—man's nearest reach to Thee;
For kinship, sonship, friendship, brotherhood
Of men—one Father—one great family;
For glimpses of the greater in the less;
For touch of Thee in wife and child and friend;
For noble self-denying motherhood;
For saintly maiden lives of rare perfume;
For little pattering feet and crooning songs;
For children's laughter, and sweet wells of truth;
For sweet child-faces and the sweet wise tongues;
For childhood's faith that lifts us near to Thee
And bows us with our own disparity;
For childhood's sweet unconscious beauty sleep;
For all that childhood teaches us of Thee;

We thank Thee, Lord!

For doubts that led us to the larger trust;
For ills to conquer; for the love that fights;
For that strong faith that vanquished axe and flame
And gave us Freedom for our heritage;
For clouds and darkness, and the still, small voice;
For sorrows bearing fruit of nobler life;
For those sore strokes that broke us at Thy feet;
For peace in strife; for gain in seeming loss;
For every loss that wrought the greater gain;

For that sweet juice from bitterness outpressed;
For all this sweet, strange paradox of life;
                                    We thank Thee, Lord!

For friends above; for friends still left below;
For the rare links invisible between;
For Thine unsearchable greatness; for the veils
Between us and the things we may not know;
For those high times when hearts take wing and rise,
And float secure above earth's mysteries;
For that wide, open avenue of prayer,
All radiant with Thy glorious promises;
For sweet hearts tuned to noblest charity;
For great hearts toiling in the outer dark;
For friendly hands stretched out in time of need;
For every gracious thought and word and deed;
                                    We thank Thee, Lord!

For songbird answering song on topmost bough;
For myriad twittering of the simpler folk;
For that sweet lark that carols up the sky;
For that low fluting on the summer night;
For distant bells that tremble on the wind;
For great round organ tones that rise and fall,
Entwined with earthly voices tuned to heaven,
And bear our hearts above the high-arched roof;
For Thy great voice that dominates the whole,
And shakes the heavens, and silences the earth;
For hearts alive to earth's sweet minstrelsies;
For souls attuned to heavenly harmonies;
For apprehension, and for ears to hear,—
                                    We thank Thee, Lord!

For that supremest token of Thy Love,—
Thyself made manifest in human flesh;
For that pure life beneath the Syrian sky—

The humble toil, the sweat, the bench, the saw,
The nails well-driven, and the work well-done;
For all its vast expansions; for the stress
Of those three mighty years;
For all He bore of our humanity;
His hunger, thirst, His homelessness and want,
His weariness that longed for well-earned rest;
For labour's high ennoblement through Him,
Who laboured with His hands for daily bread;
For Lazarus, Mary, Martha, Magdalene,
For Nazareth and Bethany;—not least
For that dark hour in lone Gethsemane;
For that high cross upraised on Calvary;
The broken seals,—the rolled-back stone—the Way,
For ever opened through His life in death;
For that brief glimpse vouchsafed within the veil;
For all His gracious life; and for His Death,
With low-bowed heads and hearts impassionate,
                              We thank Thee, Lord!

For all life's beauties, and their beauteous growth;
For Nature's laws and Thy rich providence;
For all Thy perfect processes of life;
For the minute of perfection of Thy work,
Seen and unseen, in each remotest part;
For faith, and works, and gentle charity;
For all that makes for quiet in the world;
For all that lifts man from his common rut;
For all that knits the silken bond of peace;
For all that lifts the fringes of the night,
And lights the darkened corners of the earth;
For every broken gate and sundered bar;
For every wide-flung window of the soul;
For that Thou bearest all that Thou hast made;
                              We thank Thee, Lord!

For perfect childlike confidence in Thee;
For childlike glimpses of the life to be;
For trust akin to my child's trust in me;
For hearts at rest through confidence in Thee;
For hearts triumphant in perpetual hope;
For hope victorious through past hopes fulfilled;
For mightier hopes born of the things we know;
For faith born of the things we may not know;
For hope of powers increased ten thousand fold;
For that last hope of likeness to Thyself,
When hope shall end in glorious certainty;
—With quickened hearts
That find Thee everywhere,
We thank Thee, Lord!

Te Deum of Renewals

For Thy sweet sunshine after nights of rain;
For Thy sweet balm of comfort after pain;
For Thy sweet peace that ends a long-drawn strife;
For Thy sweet rest that ends a burdened life;
For joy, dispersing sorrows as the sun
Sucks up the morning mists, and as Thy winds
Dispel the clouds and show the blue again,—
The deep, pure, tenuous, heavenly blue that seems,
In its infinity of tenderness,
Like to Thy Love, that fills all time and space
With Thy sweet Spirit's all-abounding grace;
For all Thy healing ministries,—
We thank Thee, Lord.

For hearts estranged, won back to fellowship,
And closer knit by sweet forgivenesses;

For hearts made tenderer by fortune's blows;
For souls by sorrows ripened in Thy love;
Yea, and for pain that took our pride away,
And cast us wholly on Thy charity;
For darkened ways that led us to the Light,
For blinding tears that yet renewed our sight;
For travails and perplexities of mind
Through which we wrestled, nobler life to find,—
And found, beyond our craving souls' upreach,
The wonder of the lessons Thou wouldst teach;
For dear lives salvaged from the hand of Death;
For pure souls' fiery purgings without scathe;
For answered prayers that showed Thy boundless love;
For prayers unanswered, wiser love to prove;
For all Thy leadings through life's devious ways,
With faith illumined and high heart of grace;—

We thank Thee, Lord.

Te Deum of the Years

For the life given, and for the life preserved
In peril past, and peace and joy and hope,

We thank Thee, Lord.

For every function of this mortal frame,
The mortal temple of Thy heavenly flame,
Whose complex wonders Thy great love proclaim,

We thank Thee, Lord.

For all Thy bounties through the varying years,
Granting of hopes and lightening of fears,
For Thy Great Givings, Thy Forgivings Great,

We thank Thee, Lord.

A Silent Te Deum

We thank Thee, Lord,
For all Thy Golden Silences,—
For every Sabbath from the world's turmoil;
For every respite from the stress of life;—
Silence of moorlands rolling to the skies,
Heath-purpled, bracken-clad, aflame with gorse;
Silence of gray tors crouching in the mist;
Silence of deep woods' mystic cloistered calm;
Silence of wide seas basking in the sun;
Silence of white peaks soaring to the blue;
Silence of dawnings, when, their matins sung,
The little birds do fall asleep again;
For the deep silence of high golden noons;
Silence of gloamings and the setting sun;
Silence of moonlit nights and patterned glades;
Silence of stars, magnificently still,
Yet ever chanting their Creator's skill;
For that high silence of Thine Open House,
Dim-branching roof and lofty pillared aisle,
Where burdened hearts find rest in Thee awhile;
Silence of friendship, telling more than words;
Silence of hearts, close-knitting heart to heart;
Silence of joys too wonderful for words;
Silence of sorrows, when Thou drawest near;
Silence of soul, wherein we come to Thee,
And find ourselves in Thine Immensity;
For that great silence where Thou dwell'st alone—
—Father, Spirit, Son, in One,
Keeping watch above Thine Own,—
Deep unto deep, within us sound sweet chords
Of praise beyond the reach of human words;
In our souls' silence, feeling only Thee,—
        We thank Thee, thank Thee,
          Thank Thee, Lord!

A *Te Deum* for God's Own Self

For Thine Own Self
              We thank Thee, Lord.
For this, Thy mightiest Gift of Gifts—Thyself!
That Thine Own Self Thou givest without stint,
Immeasured as Thine own eternities;
That when we seek we find Thee everywhere;
That everywhere, unseeking, still we find;
That everywhere we find ourselves in Thee,
Glad members of Thy love-linked company;
That we do find our highest selves in Thee;
In Thee do meet and find ourselves a part
Of Thy great world's unworldly throbbing heart,
Wherein Thy love pours round us like a flood
Of wise and tender father-motherhood,
Patient, long-suffering, eager-quests its own,
And yields its fullest when most called upon;
That Thine Own Self hast worn our human flesh,
And toiled, and borne, and suffered as a man;
That so Thy love is vast enough for all,—
To raise the fallen, to forgive all sin,
To heal earth's wounds, to solace every woe,
To cure the ills that suffered woes to be,
To give fresh courage to the faint of heart,
To strengthen weak and make strong souls more strong,
To be to all the Promised Comforter.

At one with Thee we find our souls in tune
With that true Soul of Life whence all Life springs;
In Thee we meet and hold communion sweet
With every other soul there entered in;
There soul greets soul though all the world divide,
There, sundered hearts are once more close allied,
And Faith and Hope and Love are sanctified;

For thought and prayer o'erleap all boundaries,
And time and space in Thee are less than nought;
Nor Death himself can interpose, since Love
Doth conquer Death, and breaks the bonds of time,
And spans the earth, and climbs the courts of Heaven.
And Thou are Love, and Very Soul of Love,
And Thou art in us, of us, with us, everywhere.

For this all-mightiest gift of Thine Own Self,
          We thank Thee, Lord!
And, since to Thee praise sweeter is than thanks,—
For Thine Own Self we praise Thee, Lord!
We praise Thee, praise Thee, praise Thee, Lord!
For thine Own Self—To Thine Own Self be praise!
The ages praise Thee,—and the days to come.
From all Thy sinless ministering hosts,—
          In service—Praise!
From all the saints by Thee from sin redeemed,—
          Still nobler praise!
From every world and creature Thou hast made,—
          Eternal praise!
For Thine Own Self, from all Thy works be praise!
Perpetual, perfect, pure, impassioned praise!—
          Praise without ceasing!
          Without ending—Praise!

X

God's To-morrow

God's To-morrow

The night is very black and grim,
—Our hearts are sick with sorrow,—
But, on the rim of the curtain dim,
A pulsing beam, a tiny gleam,
Whispers of God's To-morrow.

Beyond the night there shines a light,
—Our eyes are dim with sorrow,—
But Faith still clings, and Hope still springs,
And Love still sings of happier things,
For Life is flighting strong new wings
In search of God's To-morrow.

Life and Death

Death preys on Life,
And Life on Death doth live.
For without death
No creature that draws breath
Could live.
Strange paradox, and thought provocative,
That Life must live by death,—
That without death
Life cannot live,—
That Christ Himself,
The Lord of Life,
His life did give
That we might live.

161

Look Beyond!

Unnumbered sorrows, woes beyond belief,
A world aflame with hate and gray with grief,—
  "Look Beyond!"

This little life so short—a span at best,
And that short span a torment of unrest,—
  "Look Beyond!"

So many gone,—our bravest and our best,— .
The Golden Fields of Youth laid bare and waste,—
  "Look Beyond!"

Wrong fills the world with foul iniquity,
"God's grace is more than man's obliquity,—
  Look Beyond!"

What can Life give to recompense such loss?
"Christ's path of sorrow led Him to the cross,—
  Look Beyond!"

Before these horrors Hope and Love are dumb.
"Hold to your Faith! God's best is still to come,—
  Look Beyond!"

There Is No Death

There is no death.—
They only truly live
Who pass into the life beyond, and see
This earth is but a school preparative
For larger ministry.

There is no death
To those whose hearts are set
On higher things than this life doth afford;
How shall their passing leave one least regret,
Who go to join their Lord?

Quoted in part

Comfort Ye!

I

In that sweet after-life,
When time is done,
And living hearts again are one
In perfect union,
You shall look back and say,—
"And did I mourn that he
Passed on in front of me
By just one day?
The time indeed seemed long to me,
And hushed my song in misery;
But, in the light of this eternity,
'Twas but a span,—just a short winter's day,—
Soon past
And by these present joys far overpassed."

163

II

I see their shining eyes,
Their glad and eager faces,
Waiting to welcome us
To the heavenly places.
And how shall we complain
Of our own loss and pain,
When unto them we know the change
Is all eternal gain?

III

Ah—how we miss him—
Every hour of every day!
Life, since he went, has been a gray
Dull way, wherein we stray
Neighboured with grief, and blinded with dismay.

Never to see him more!
To hear his voice!—to see his face again!
Lord, it is sore beyond our ken,—
How shall our hearts endure
Discomfiture so great and such vast forfeiture?

And yet, our faith dare not gainsay
Thy love in taking him away.
Such good is his, such perfect bliss,
How could we wish him back in this
Small world of grim perplexities?

And, of a truth, at times he feels so near,—
Nearer in very deed
Than when we had him here,—
That we are comforted.
We cast despair and put away our fear.

164

We shall not see him here again;
To us he may not come;
But when at last we shall attain
The heavenly place, be his dear face
The first to greet us in Thy grace
And bid us "Welcome Home!"

Shortened Lives

To us it seemed his life was too soon done,
Ended, indeed, while scarcely yet begun;
God, with His clearer vision, saw that he
Was ready for a larger ministry.

Just so we thought of Him, whose life below
Was so full-charged with bitterness and woe,
Our clouded vision would have crowned Him King,
He chose the lowly way of suffering.

Remember, too, how short His life on earth,—
But three-and-thirty years 'twixt death and birth.
And of those years but three whereof we know,
Yet those three years immortal seed did sow.

It is not tale of years that tells the whole
Of man's success or failure, but the soul
He brings to them, the songs he sings to them,
The steadfast gaze he fixes on the goal.

Help Me, O Father God

Help me, O Father God,
To do good work for Thee,
And when Thou deem'st my work is done
Take me home speedily.

Just touch me with Thy hand
And instant bid me come,
And joyfully I'll speed, O Lord,
To meet Thy "Welcome Home!"

After Work

Lord, when Thou seest that my work is done,
Let me not linger on,
With failing powers,
Adown the weary hours,—
A workless worker in a world of work.
But, with a word,
Just bid me home,
And I will come
Right gladly,—
Yea, right gladly
Will I come.

A Dieu! and Au Revoir!

As you love me, let there be
No mourning when I go,—
No tearful eyes,
No hopeless sighs,
No woe,—nor even sadness!
Indeed I would not have you sad,
For I myself shall be full glad,
With the high triumphant gladness
Of a soul made free
Of God's sweet liberty.

—No windows darkened;
For my own
Will be flung wide, as ne'er before,
To catch the radiant inpour
Of Love that shall in full atone
For all the ills that I have done;
And the good things left undone;
—No voices hushed;
My own, full-flushed
With an immortal hope, will rise
In ecstasies of new-born bliss
And joyful melodies.

Rather, of your sweet courtesy,
Rejoice with me
At my soul's loosing from captivity.
Wish me "Bon voyage!"
As you do a friend
Whose joyous visit finds its happy end.
And bid me both "A Dieu!"
And "Au revoir!"
Since, though I come no more,

167

I shall be waiting there to greet you,
At His Door.

And, as the feet of the bearers tread
The ways I trod,
Think not of me as dead,
But rather—
"Happy, thrice happy, he whose course is sped!
He has gone home—to God,
His Father!"

Nightfall

Fold up the tent!
The sun is in the West.
Tomorrow my untented soul will range
Among the blest.
    And I am well content,
    For what is sent, is sent,
    And God knows best.

Fold up the tent,
And speed the parting guest!
The night draws on, though night and day
  are one
On this long quest.
    This house was only lent
    For my apprenticement—
    What is, is best.

Fold up the tent!
Its slack ropes all undone,

Its pole all broken, and its cover rent,—
Its work is done.
    But mine—tho' spoiled and spent
    Mine earthly tenement—
    Is but begun.

Fold up the tent!
Its tenant would be gone,
To fairer skies than mortal eyes
May look upon.
    All that I loved has passed,
    And left me at the last
    Alone!—Alone!

Fold up the tent!
Above the mountain's crest,
I hear a clear voice calling, calling clear,—
"To rest! To rest!"
    And I am glad to go,
    For the sweet oil is low,
    And rest is best!

Index of Titles

Index of First Lines